Reading Achievement
Comprehension Activities to Promote Essential Reading Skills

Grade 4

by
Jennifer Moore

Table of Contents

Introduction 3
Pretests 4-7
Answer Key for Pretests 8
Following Directions 9-10
Finding the Main Idea 11-12
Finding Facts 13-14
Figurative Language 15-16
Drawing Conclusions 17-18
Reading Charts 19
Reading Tables 20
Reading Graphs 21
A Beautiful Fiber 22-23
Eat Your Veggies! 24-25
Tennis, Anyone? 26-27
Hello, Mr. Bell 28-29
Zachary Taylor 30-31
Dolly and Brittany 32-33
Aunt Mary's Baby 34-35
July 36-37
Jacques Cousteau 38-39
Hawaii 40
Portugal 41
Basketball Camp 42-43
House Hunting 44-45
Another Use for Seeds 46-47
Holiday Shopping 48
Mr. FBI 49
Accidental Inventions 50
Rain 51
Leave It to the Leaves 52-53
Nancy's Office 54-55
The Comforts of Home 56-57
A New Way to Communicate 58-59
Dad's Surprise 60-61
Sam and Matt 62-63
Hockey 64
Happiness 65
Washing Windows 66-67
Ancient Wonders 68-69
Heidi's Notebook 70-71
Lunar Landing 72-73
The Painting on the Ceiling 74-75
Honeybees 76-78
Answer Key 79-96

Introduction

Welcome to the **Reading Achievement** series! Each book in this series is designed to reinforce the reading skills appropriate for each grade level and to encourage high-level thinking skills. Because reading is an essential part of all disciplines, mastery of these skills can help students succeed in all academic areas. In addition, experiencing success in reading can increase a student's self-esteem and motivate him or her to read more, both in and out of the classroom.

Each **Reading Achievement** book offers challenging questions for students to answer in response to a variety of grade-level appropriate passages. Various types of reading passages are represented in this book, including fiction, nonfiction, poetry, charts and graphs, recipes, and crossword puzzles. The format and questions are similar to those found on standardized reading tests. The experience students gain from answering questions in this format may help increase their test scores. In addition, these exercises can be used to enhance your school-adopted reading program, to individualize instruction, to provide extra practice for home schoolers, or to review skills between grades.

The following reading skills are covered within this book:

- **comprehension**
- **critical thinking**
- **fact or opinion**
- **figurative language**
- **following directions**
- **main ideas/details**
- **true or false**
- **vocabulary**

Each **Reading Achievement** book contains additional features to enhance usability. Four pretests, in standardized test format, have been included at the beginning of each book. The pretests have been designed so that they may be used individually, as four stand-alone tests, or in groups. Another convenient feature is a scoring box on each activity page. This scoring box can be programmed to suit your specific classroom and student needs with total problems, total correct, and score.

Read the passage and answer the questions. Circle the letter beside the correct answer.

Oysters are sea creatures that are valuable as food and for the pearls they produce. Most oysters come from areas in the North Atlantic. They like quiet, shallow waters like bays and river mouths. They are sometimes grown as a crop. Fishermen locate good places to plant the seed oysters. These places are called beds. They clean the trash out of the beds, and then they plant the seed oysters. They feed and care for the oysters until they are ready to harvest.

Oysters like warm waters. In southern areas, they grow to full size in two to three years. In cooler northern waters, it takes about four years for them to grow.

Pearl oysters do not belong to the same family as the oysters we eat. A pearl may be found in an oyster that can be eaten, but it isn't a good pearl. Fine pearls come from a different kind of oyster called a "pearl oyster." They grow in warm waters in southern oceans.

1. What are two products that we get from oysters?
   A. food and pearls
   C. pearls and diamonds
   B. food and beds
   D. food and cool water

2. How long does it take for an oyster to grow to full size in northern waters?
   A. one year
   C. three years
   B. two years
   D. four years

3. In this story the word "beds" means:
   A. places to sleep
   C. places that fishermen grow oysters
   B. places to find pearls
   D. gardens

4. Where are most oysters found?
   A. southern seas
   C. Northern Atlantic
   B. grocery store
   D. on the beach

5. Oysters grow best in:
   A. warm water and busy lakes
   C. quiet, shallow bays and warm water
   B. quiet, shallow bays and cool water
   D. mountain rivers

6. When a fisherman wants to grow oysters as a crop, what does he do first?
   A. harvest them
   C. plant seed oysters
   B. feed and care for them
   D. locate a good bed and clean it

7. If you find a pearl in an oyster, you should probably:
   A. take it straight to a jeweler
   C. sell it
   B. eat it
   D. keep it as a souvenir

4

Total Problems: _____   Total Correct: _____   Score: _____

Read the recipe and answer the questions. Circle the letter beside the correct answer.

Caramel Corn Snacks

$\frac{1}{2}$ cup butter

1 cup packed, light brown sugar

$\frac{1}{4}$ cup light corn syrup

$\frac{1}{2}$ teaspoon salt

$\frac{1}{2}$ teaspoon vanilla extract

$\frac{1}{4}$ teaspoon baking soda

3 quarts unsalted, popped popcorn

1 cup salted peanuts (optional)

In a 1 $\frac{1}{2}$-quart saucepan, combine butter, brown sugar, corn syrup, and salt. Bring mixture to a boil, stirring constantly. Boil over medium heat without stirring for 5 minutes. Remove from heat; stir in vanilla and baking soda. In a large bowl, gradually pour hot syrup over popcorn, mixing well to coat the corn. Place popcorn in greased 17 x 12 x 2-inch pan. Bake, uncovered, at 300 degrees for 30 minutes, stirring the popcorn after 15 minutes. Remove from oven; cool completely in pan. Loosen popcorn with a spatula; break into pieces. Stir in peanuts. Store in a covered container.

1. When the popcorn mixture is in the oven, what does the recipe tell you to do?
   - A.   wash the saucepan
   - B.   stir in the peanuts
   - C.   pour hot syrup over it
   - D.   stir it after 15 minutes

2. What does the word "optional" mean in this recipe?
   - A.   You can add the peanuts if you want to, but you don't have to.
   - B.   It will ruin the snack if you leave out the peanuts.
   - C.   You can use peanuts instead of popcorn.
   - D.   If you add peanuts, you should call it something different.

3. What does the word "combine" mean in this recipe?
   - A.   take the ingredients out of the cupboard
   - B.   mix the ingredients together
   - C.   taste the ingredients
   - D.   bake the ingredients

4. What does the recipe tell you to do first?
   - A.   remove from heat; stir in vanilla and baking soda
   - B.   loosen popcorn with a spatula; break into pieces
   - C.   bring mixture to a boil, stirring constantly
   - D.   combine butter, brown sugar, corn syrup, and salt

5. What is the last thing the recipe tells you to do?
   - A.   store in a covered container
   - B.   bake it for 30 minutes
   - C.   pour hot syrup over the popcorn
   - D.   boil it for 5 minutes without stirring

Total Problems:	Total Correct:	Score:

Review the chart and answer the questions. Circle the letter beside the correct answer.

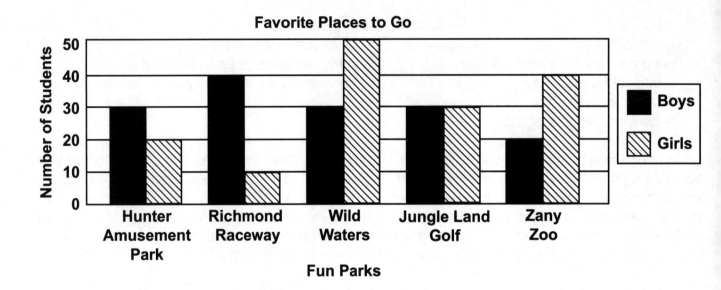

1. From this chart, we can tell:
   A. how many boys and how many girls like each place best
   B. how much each place costs to visit
   C. where each place is located
   D. what there is to do at each place

2. Which place do both boys and girls like equally?
   A. Zany Zoo
   B. Richmond Raceway
   C. Wild Waters
   D. Jungle Land Golf

3. Which place is most popular with boys?
   A. Hunter Amusement Park
   B. Jungle Land Golf
   C. Richmond Raceway
   D. Hunter Amusement Park

4. Which place is the most popular among boys and girls together?
   A. Hunter Amusement Park
   B. Jungle Land Golf
   C. Wild Waters
   D. Zany Zoo

6

Total Problems: _____   Total Correct: _____   Score: _____

Read the paragraph and answer the questions. Circle the letter beside the correct answer.

What happened to the Fridge? William "the Refrigerator" Perry played professional football from the mid-1980s through the mid-1990s for the Chicago Bears, the Philadelphia Eagles, and the London Monarch. One sportswriter said that he could move a line like a bulldozer. He described a game where the Fridge picked up another player who was holding the ball and threw him over a pile of players into the end zone. The referee called a penalty, but no one could get too angry with him. Who else could do that? Perry is retired now and lives in South Carolina. He and his father-in-law own a masonry business, and Perry lays bricks and cinder blocks. He says he likes the blocks because they fit in his hand better than a football. He is married and has three children. In his spare time, he likes to go fishing.

1. The Fridge's real name is:
    A. Refrigerator   B. William Perry
    C. William Monarch   D. Refrigerator Perry

2. Refrigerator Perry played:
    A. professional hockey   B. professional baseball
    C. professional football   D. professional fishing

3. Which of the following does not tell something about his size?
    A. He likes blocks because they fit better in his hand.
    B. His nickname is the Fridge or Refrigerator.
    C. He could move a line like a bulldozer.
    D. He is married and has three children.

4. When the sportswriter said that he could move a line like a bulldozer, he meant that:
    A. He drives a bulldozer in his business.
    B. He pushed the other players out of the way.
    C. He was fast.
    D. He picked up other players.

5. Refrigerator Perry played football for approximately how many years?
    A. 10
    B. 5
    C. 20
    D. 1

6. Who was Perry's father-in-law?
    A. Perry's father   B. Perry's uncle
    C. Perry's grandfather   D. Perry's wife's father

Total Problems:	Total Correct:	Score:

Name _____   **Pretest**

Read the passage and answer the questions. Circle the letter beside the correct answer.

Oysters are sea creatures that are valuable as food and for the pearls they produce. Most oysters come from areas in the North Atlantic. They like quiet, shallow waters like bays and river mouths. They are sometimes grown as a crop. Fishermen locate good places to plant the seed oysters. These places are called beds. They clean the trash out of the beds, and then they plant the seed oysters. They feed and care for the oysters until they are ready to harvest.

Oysters like warm waters. In southern areas, they grow to full size in two to three years. In cooler northern waters, it takes about four years for them to grow.

Pearl oysters do not belong to the same family as the oysters we eat. A pearl may be found in an oyster that can be eaten, but it isn't a good pearl. Fine pearls come from a different kind of oyster called a "pearl oyster." They grow in warm waters in southern oceans.

1. What are two products that we get from oysters?
   A. food and pearls
   B. food and beds
   C. pearls and diamonds
   D. food and cool water

2. How long does it take for an oyster to grow to full size in northern waters?
   A. one year
   B. two years
   C. three years
   D. four years

3. In this story the word "beds" means:
   A. places to sleep
   B. places to find pearls
   C. places that fishermen grow oysters
   D. gardens

4. Where are most oysters found?
   A. southern seas
   B. grocery store
   C. Northern Atlantic
   D. on the beach

5. Oysters grow best in:
   A. warm water and busy lakes
   B. quiet, shallow bays and cool water
   C. quiet, shallow bays and warm water
   D. mountain rivers

6. When a fisherman wants to grow oysters as a crop, what does he do first?
   A. harvest them
   B. feed and care for them
   C. plant seed oysters
   D. locate a good bed and clean it

7. If you find a pearl in an oyster, you should probably:
   A. take it straight to a jeweler
   B. eat it
   C. sell it
   D. keep it as a souvenir

④ | Total Problems: | Total Correct: | Score: |

© Carson-Dellosa CD-2203

Name _____   **Pretest**

Read the recipe and answer the questions. Circle the letter beside the correct answer.

Caramel Corn Snacks

½ cup butter	¼ teaspoon baking soda
1 cup packed, light brown sugar	3 quarts unsalted, popped popcorn
¼ cup light corn syrup	1 cup salted peanuts (optional)
½ teaspoon salt	
½ teaspoon vanilla extract	

In a 1 ½-quart saucepan, combine butter, brown sugar, corn syrup, and salt. Bring mixture to a boil, stirring constantly. Boil over medium heat without stirring for 5 minutes. Remove from heat; stir in vanilla and baking soda. In a large bowl, gradually pour hot syrup over popcorn, mixing well to coat the corn. Place popcorn in greased 17 x 12 x 2-inch pan. Bake, uncovered, at 300 degrees for 30 minutes, stirring the popcorn after 15 minutes. Remove from oven; cool completely in pan. Loosen popcorn with a spatula; break into pieces. Stir in peanuts. Store in a covered container.

1. When the popcorn mixture is in the oven, what does the recipe tell you to do?
   A. wash the saucepan
   B. stir in the peanuts
   C. pour hot syrup over it
   D. stir it after 15 minutes

2. What does the word "optional" mean in this recipe?
   A. You can add the peanuts if you want to, but you don't have to.
   B. It will ruin the snack if you leave out the peanuts.
   C. You can use peanuts instead of popcorn.
   D. If you add peanuts, you should call it something different.

3. What does the word "combine" mean in this recipe?
   A. take the ingredients out of the cupboard
   B. mix the ingredients together
   C. taste the ingredients
   D. bake the ingredients

4. What does the recipe tell you to do first?
   A. remove from heat; stir in vanilla and baking soda
   B. loosen popcorn with a spatula; break into pieces
   C. bring mixture to a boil, stirring constantly
   D. combine butter, brown sugar, corn syrup, and salt

5. What is the last thing the recipe tells you to do?
   A. store in a covered container
   B. bake it for 30 minutes
   C. pour hot syrup over the popcorn
   D. boil it for 5 minutes without stirring

© Carson-Dellosa CD-2203

| Total Problems: | Total Correct: | Score: | ⑤

Name _____   **Pretest**

Review the chart and answer the questions. Circle the letter beside the correct answer.

Favorite Places to Go

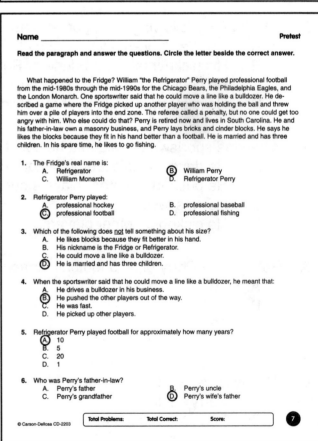

Fun Parks

Boys / Girls

Hunter Amusement Park, Richmond Raceway, Wild Waters, Jungle Land Golf, Zany Zoo

1. From this chart, we can tell:
   A. how many boys and how many girls like each place best
   B. how much each place costs to visit
   C. where each place is located
   D. what there is to do at each place

2. Which place do both boys and girls like equally?
   A. Zany Zoo
   B. Richmond Raceway
   C. Wild Waters
   D. Jungle Land Golf

3. Which place is most popular with boys?
   A. Hunter Amusement Park
   B. Jungle Land Golf
   C. Richmond Raceway
   D. Hunter Amusement Park

4. Which place is the most popular among boys and girls together?
   A. Hunter Amusement Park
   B. Jungle Land Golf
   C. Wild Waters
   D. Zany Zoo

⑥ | Total Problems: | Total Correct: | Score: |

© Carson-Dellosa CD-2203

Name _____   **Pretest**

Read the paragraph and answer the questions. Circle the letter beside the correct answer.

What happened to the Fridge? William "the Refrigerator" Perry played professional football from the mid-1980s through the mid-1990s for the Chicago Bears, the Philadelphia Eagles, and the London Monarch. One sportswriter said that he could move a line like a bulldozer. He described a game where the Fridge picked up another player who was holding the ball and threw him over a pile of players into the end zone. The referee called a penalty, but no one could get too angry with him. Who else could do that? Perry is retired now and lives in South Carolina. He and his father-in-law own a masonry business, and Perry lays bricks and cinder blocks. He says he likes the blocks because they fit in his hand better than a football. He is married and has three children. In his spare time, he likes to go fishing.

1. The Fridge's real name is:
   A. Refrigerator
   B. William Perry
   C. William Monarch
   D. Refrigerator Perry

2. Refrigerator Perry played:
   A. professional hockey
   B. professional baseball
   C. professional football
   D. professional fishing

3. Which of the following does not tell something about his size?
   A. He likes blocks because they fit better in his hand.
   B. His nickname is the Fridge or Refrigerator.
   C. He could move a line like a bulldozer.
   D. He is married and has three children.

4. When the sportswriter said that he could move a line like a bulldozer, he meant that:
   A. He drives a bulldozer in his business.
   B. He pushed the other players out of the way.
   C. He was fast.
   D. He picked up other players.

5. Refrigerator Perry played football for approximately how many years?
   A. 10
   B. 5
   C. 20
   D. 1

6. Who was Perry's father-in-law?
   A. Perry's father
   B. Perry's uncle
   C. Perry's grandfather
   D. Perry's wife's father

© Carson-Dellosa CD-2203

| Total Problems: | Total Correct: | Score: | ⑦

Name _____

In the grid below, find the three items that are alike and in a straight row horizontally, vertically, or diagonally. Draw an oval ring around all three items. Write an "x" on the items that are not like the items in the ring. Write the number of different items that are used in the puzzle. Make a puzzle like this for a friend and explain the directions to him or her.

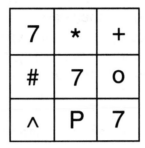

Number of items: _____

Answer the questions below. Circle the letter beside the correct answer.

1. The instructions direct you to find three like items in a:
    A.   row
    B.   box
    C.   ring
    D.   square

2. The second task you are asked to perform is to:
    A.   find three like items
    B.   write an "x" on the other items
    C.   draw a ring around the three like items
    D.   make a game for a friend

3. Last, the directions instruct you to:
    A.   make a puzzle like this for a friend
    B.   draw a puzzle with nine items
    C.   draw a ring around the like items
    D.   find the items unlike the others

4. How many different items were used in the puzzle? _____

5. In what direction did the three like items lie?
    A.   horizontal
    B.   vertical
    C.   diagonal

Total Problems: Total Correct: Score:

9

Read the paragraph and answer the questions. Circle the letter beside the correct answer.

Making Sandwiches

Sara and Jane made peanut butter and jelly sandwiches for a picnic. First, they gathered all of the ingredients they would need and two knives. Next, they took several slices of bread from the bag and placed them on paper plates. Then, they each spread peanut butter on one slice of bread. Next, they each took another slice of bread and spread grape jelly on it. Then, they put the pieces of bread together to make two sandwiches. Finally, they sliced the sandwiches in half and wrapped them in plastic wrap. They made the rest of the sandwiches the same way and finished packing their basket for the picnic.

1. What did the girls do right after spreading the grape jelly on the bread?
   A. They sliced the sandwiches.
   B. They placed the sandwiches on a paper plate.
   C. The girls put the pieces of bread together, making two sandwiches.
   D. They packed the picnic basket.

2. What was the very first thing the girls did?
   A. spread peanut butter on a slice of bread
   B. took out two slices of bread
   C. gathered the ingredients
   D. took out paper plates and a picnic basket

3. What was the last thing the girls did?
   A. made peanut butter and jelly sandwiches
   B. finished packing their picnic basket
   C. ate the sandwiches they had made
   D. selected the pieces of bread

4. Choose the sequence that best describes the girls' actions.
   A. slice sandwiches, spread peanut butter, pack the basket
   B. pack the basket, get the ingredients, spread the jelly
   C. get the bread, spread the jelly, spread the peanut butter
   D. spread peanut butter, slice the sandwiches, pack the basket

Total Problems: _____   Total Correct: _____   Score: _____

Read the paragraphs and answer the questions. Circle the letter beside the correct answer.

Thunderstorm

Sam and Thomas were playing catch in Sam's yard when a loud clap of thunder exploded across the sky. This frightened the boys, so they ran inside. Hard rain soon started to hit the house. Sam's mother was coming downstairs to meet the boys when suddenly all of the lights in the house went out, the television went blank, and the kitchen appliances shut off. "Oh no! The power is out," said Sam. "This is going to ruin our plans for a baseball game!"

1. What is the main idea of the paragraph?
   - A. It is better to be with a friend when the weather is bad.
   - B. Playing outside is always dangerous for children.
   - C. A thunderstorm was beginning to start in Sam's neighborhood.
   - D. Always play catch away from the windows of a house.

Melissa's Guitar

Melissa's father gave her a guitar for her ninth birthday. She was very excited about learning how to play it. She would often stand in front of her bedroom mirror pretending to be on stage performing for a huge crowd. She began taking guitar lessons from a local music teacher. She surprised her teacher because she learned so quickly. Melissa played some songs she learned at her school talent show. Her friends were also surprised at how well she played. Some of her friends predicted that Melissa would become a rock star one day.

2. What is the main idea of the paragraph?
   - A. Girls can play the guitar as well as boys.
   - B. Melissa loved to play the guitar.
   - C. Most musicians learn to play the guitar when they are young.
   - D. Everyone can play a musical instrument.

Read the paragraphs and answer the questions. Circle the letter beside the correct answer.

Molly's Birthday

Molly was going to be ten years old on Wednesday. She was very excited about this birthday because she was going to be in the double digits! At school she scribbled all different sizes and kinds of "tens" in her notebook. She wrote some numbers really big and some fat. Then, she colored them in with a marker. Her party was already planned, and she had invited ten friends! It was going to last until ten o'clock Saturday night because she had invited her friends to a movie. The movie would be over at ten o'clock. Molly thought this was going to be the neatest birthday she had ever had.

1. What is the main idea of the paragraph?
    A.   Birthday parties should include a movie.
    B.   Molly is going to get her birthday wish.
    C.   Planning a party can be hard.
    D.   Molly was excited about her birthday.

Ellie

Ellie was a little black dog who lived with the Sanders family. Mr. and Mrs. Sanders had two children, Mark and Amy. The children loved Ellie very much. Mark liked to play ball with Ellie in the backyard. Amy liked to take Ellie for walks after school. They loved to have her wake them up in the mornings by jumping on their beds and licking their faces. Ellie was a lot of fun to have around! Sometimes Mr. Sanders would pick up treats for Ellie from the pet store on his way home from work. Ellie would greet Mr. Sanders at the door every evening when he came home.

2. What is the main idea of the paragraph?
    A.   Pets are the best companions for children.
    B.   Ellie was a great dog for the Sanders family.
    C.   Mr. Sanders was a very good pet owner.
    D.   Dogs are better pets than cats.

Total Problems: Total Correct: Score:

Read the paragraph and answer the questions. Write an "x" in the blank next to each statement below that is a fact from the paragraph.

The Human Body

The human body is made up of many systems. Each bodily system has a special function to carry out using specific organs and tissues. It is important for good health that all of the systems work together. Each system is made up of one primary organ and other supporting parts. These parts together carry out major body functions. For example, the heart is the primary organ that controls the circulatory system. The blood flows through the veins by way of the heart. All of the organs in these systems are vital for the body to work properly. Organs are so important that doctors work to teach people how to properly care for them and their bodies.

1. _____ The body needs the organs to carry out special functions.

2. _____ More people have problems with the circulatory system than the digestive system.

3. _____ The heart is the primary organ in the circulatory system.

4. _____ Good health exists when all of the systems of the body are working properly.

5. _____ The human body is made up of only one system of organs and tissues.

Read the paragraph and answer the questions. Write an "x" in the blank next to each statement below that is a fact from the paragraph.

William Shakespeare

William Shakespeare is considered the world's greatest literary mind by many notable authorities. Born in England, Shakespeare received little formal schooling. He became fond of the theater when his father's shop was near an old chapel that often opened its doors to traveling actors. William attended some of the shows and enjoyed hearing the lines spoken from the stage. Shakespeare wrote mostly poetry early in his career. He is famous for his sonnets and long narrative poems. Shakespeare became wealthy as a result of his craft. Tax records in England show that at one time he was required to pay nearly five pounds in property tax because he owned so much land. During that time, five pounds was a large sum of money.

1. _____ William Shakespeare was never formally educated.

2. _____ Shakespeare made money from his works of literature.

3. _____ Shakespeare's father was an actor.

4. _____ Many of Shakespeare's works include poetry.

5. _____ Shakespeare lived in Scotland.

Total Problems: **Total Correct:**   **Score:**

Read the paragraphs and answer the questions. Circle the letter beside the correct answer.

The Science Project

Mandy and Allison decided to do a science fair project together. They selected the topic of photosynthesis. The girls included the three critical science steps: create a hypothesis, follow a procedure, and reach a conclusion. They knew that it would take a long time to complete their science project because each step needed to be carefully carried out. The girls were as busy as bees for the next three weeks as they prepared the project. When they had finished, the girls were very pleased with their work and felt like they had a great chance at winning a ribbon.

1. Why did the author use the phrase "as busy as bees"?
   A. Bees are good subjects for science projects.
   B. People can learn from how bees work.
   C. Bees have certain jobs within colonies and are known as hard workers.
   D. Working reminds the author of bees.

The Bike Ride

David and Lee had been riding their bikes almost all morning on Saturday. They left David's house at nine-thirty A.M. and met their friend Brian for a ride in the park. The three boys raced each other through the trails in the park and up the hill toward Lee's house. Only once during their ride did they stop to rest. Finally, Brian looked at his watch and noticed he had a baseball game in forty-five minutes. After they said good-bye, they all rode off in different directions. David wheeled into his driveway and parked his bike by the back door. He went in the house and found his mother making lunch. "I'm as hungry as a horse," said David. "Thanks for making lunch, Mom!"

2. Why did the author use the phrase "I'm as hungry as a horse"?
   A. Horses are usually hungry after a day of work.
   B. Horses are large animals and they eat a lot.
   C. Boys and horses like the same foods.
   D. David wants a horse of his own someday.

Total Problems:	Total Correct:	Score:

15

Read the paragraphs and answer the questions. Circle the letter beside the correct answer.

Sandy's Birthday Party

Sandy and her mother were planning Sandy's tenth birthday party. They had chosen a sports theme and had already selected the date for the party. As they continued with their plans, Sandy noticed her soccer schedule had come in the mail. She began looking over the information from her coach and saw that the dates for the tournament had been set. The tournament was going to begin on her birthday! She showed the schedule to her mother and began talking about changing her party plans. It was a good thing she noticed the conflict in the schedule because her mother was about to print the invitations on the computer. "Wow, I would have been in a pickle if I hadn't noticed that tournament date!" said Sandy. She and her mom settled on another date for her party, and they printed her invitations.

1. Why did the author use the phrase "I would have been in a pickle"?
   A. Sandy wanted to have pickles at her birthday party.
   B. Sandy's mother was going to help her make pickles for her birthday party.
   C. It means that someone is in a bad or conflicting situation.
   D. People who get things confused often have more trouble later.

The Hiking Trip

Nicholas was excited about his upcoming hiking trip. He carefully planned for several days before the trip, making sure to take everything he would need. Finally, the day of the trip arrived. He and the other kids in the Outdoor Club loaded the van with all of their gear and headed for the mountains. They spent all of their daytime hours hiking. The group stopped to set up camp each evening at about five-thirty p.m. When the sun came up on the third day, Nicholas was sleeping like a log. He was awakened by some of the other club members as they were packing up their sleeping bags and having breakfast. Today was the trip down the mountain. Nicholas had enjoyed his adventure, but he was growing tired. He was happy to be going home.

2. Why did the author use the phrase "sleeping like a log"?
   A. Logs are motionless, and the phrase implies how still and quiet he was sleeping.
   B. Boys usually pretend to be other things to trick their friends.
   C. Most hikers sleep near logs so it is easy to make a campsite at night.
   D. Everyone was sleeping, including the trees.

Total Problems: Total Correct: Score:

Name _____

Read the paragraphs and answer the questions. Circle the letter beside the correct answer.

A New Adventure

Molly and Jake got up early. They were so excited about the new year ahead. They had chosen their clothes the night before and packed their book bags. After getting dressed, they hurried downstairs to the kitchen to prepare their breakfast. Jake chose cereal, and Molly wanted a bagel. Soon their mother came into the kitchen. She poured a cup of coffee for herself and listened to her children chatter with excitement about their new adventure. Mrs. Murphy reminded her children to brush their teeth. Finally, the bus came down the street. Jake and Molly hurried out to greet it and waved good-bye to their mother.

1. Why do you think Jake and Molly were excited?
   A. It was a holiday.
   B. It was snowing.
   C. They were going on a trip.
   D. It was the first day of school.

Unpacking

Everyone in the Miller household was busy unpacking boxes and unwrapping treasures that had been in storage for the past eleven months. Susie and John were most excited when Dad began instructing the workers where to place the den furniture. This den was much larger than their old one. Susie and John hurried from room to room to join in on any action they could find. They helped their mother arrange their bedroom furniture and place boxes of clothes beside the closet doors so they could be unpacked. The atmosphere was hectic yet happy for several hours. The family ate pizza later that evening and then went to sleep.

2. What were the family members in the paragraph most likely doing?
   A. decorating their house for a party
   B. preparing for a garage sale
   C. moving into their new house
   D. getting ready for the first day of school

Total Problems: Total Correct: Score: 17

Read the paragraphs and answer the questions. Circle the letter beside the correct answer.

A Hot Summer Day

Tammy ran into the house after a long, hot afternoon of playing with her friend Sheila. Her mother was beginning to prepare dinner. Tammy liked the smell of hamburger meat cooking in the kitchen. It was Friday, and it had been a great day. Tammy was very thirsty, and her mother asked her if she wanted a drink. "Yes, please," Tammy said. Her mother took a glass from the cabinet and filled it from a bottle she took from the refrigerator. Tammy quickly drank the cool, sweet brown beverage and laughed as the bubbles of carbonation tickled her top lip. This was very refreshing. When she finished her drink, she headed to her room to read before dinner.

1. What was Tammy most likely drinking?
    A. water
    B. soda
    C. apple juice
    D. orange juice

A Surprise

Laurie and Jay had just gotten home from school when their mother met them in the yard and told them about a surprise. She took them to the backyard, and they noticed a large cardboard box sitting on the patio. The children started to walk toward the box and noticed that the sides were moving slightly. Jay heard a faint whimper coming from the box. The children ran to the box and looked inside. They saw a furry white animal in the corner of the box.

2. What do you think the children saw in the box?
    A. a bird
    B. a puppy
    C. a cotton ball
    D. a lizard

Total Problems: _____   Total Correct: _____   Score: _____

Use the information in the chart to answer the questions. Write the answers on the lines provided below.

10 Tokens	30 Tokens	50 Tokens
key chain	stuffed animal	sunglasses
note pad	ball	paint set
bubble gum	mouse pad	disguise kit
whistle	joke book	spray string
popcorn	jumbo pencil	action figure
stickers	puzzle	sparkle pen

1. How many tokens are required for a stuffed animal? _____

2. If Janet has 60 tokens, how many paint sets can she get? _____

3. Meg has 50 tokens. Can she get a whistle and sunglasses? _____

4. Sandy has 80 tokens. Can she get a note pad and spray string? _____

5. How many tokens are needed to get a key chain and a sparkle pen? _____

6. How many tokens in all are needed for a puzzle, bubble gum, and popcorn? _____

7. Jake has 90 tokens. Can he get 2 stuffed animals and an action figure? _____

8. Robin has 40 tokens. How many 30-token items can she get? _____

9. Lynn has 20 tokens just for popcorn. How many bags can she get? _____

10. Dan has 50 tokens. If he gets spray string, will he have any tokens left over? _____

| Total Problems: | Total Correct: | Score: |

Name _____

Use the information in the table to answer the questions. Write the answers on the lines provided below.

Average Monthly Temperatures					
June	July	Aug.	Sept.	Oct.	Nov.
88°	85°	96°	81°	78°	75°

1. Which month(s) was cooler than October? _____

2. Which month(s) was warmer than September? _____

3. What month had an average temperature of 96°? _____

4. How many months were cooler than June? _____

5. Which month had an average temperature of 85°? _____

6. Which month(s) was 3 degrees cooler than June? _____

Total Problems: _____ Total Correct: _____ Score: _____

Use the information in the graph to answer the questions. Write the answers on the lines provided below.

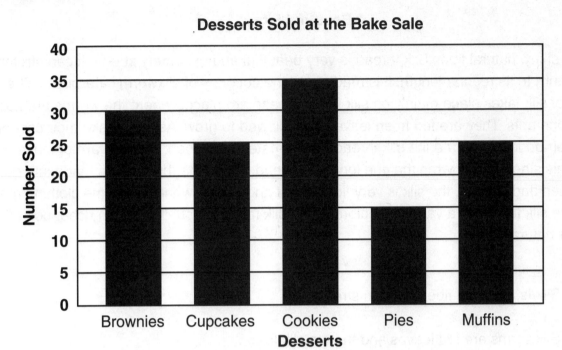

Desserts Sold at the Bake Sale

1. How many pies were sold at the bake sale? _____

2. How many brownies were sold at the bake sale? _____

3. Which item at the bake sale was the most popular? _____

4. Which item at the bake sale was the least popular? _____

5. How many more brownies were sold than muffins? _____

6. How many fewer pies were sold than cookies? _____

7. Of the cookies and cupcakes, which sold more? _____

8. Of the muffins and pies, which sold more? _____

9. Twenty-five pieces each were sold of which two desserts? _____

Total Problems:	Total Correct:	Score:

Read the paragraph. Write a "T" in the blank next to each statement below that is true. Write an "F" if the statement is false.

A Beautiful Fiber

Silk is a shiny, natural fiber. Silk thread is very beautiful and extremely strong. It can stretch and then return to its regular length. It is made from the cocoons of silkworm caterpillars. The production of silk takes place mainly on silk farms. These are places where the worms are kept in clean environments. They are fed fresh leaves and allowed to grow. As they make their cocoons, they use their bodies to create the silk threads that create the cocoon. The silk farmers take a cocoon at this stage and unwrap the one long silk thread. When the threads are made into garments for men and women, the silk is very lightweight and resists wrinkling. Some clothing manufacturers dye silk fabrics in a variety of colors. Dyed silk fabric is usually a much richer color than that of other natural fibers.

1. _____ Silk is a natural fiber that can stretch.

2. _____ Silkworms are fed leaves and fruit on silk farms.

3. _____ The silk thread comes from the silkworm's cocoon.

4. _____ Silk can be dyed and usually appears richer than other fabrics similarly dyed.

5. _____ Clothing stores dye their silk fabrics.

Total Problems: _____   Total Correct: _____   Score: _____

Name _____

Refer to the paragraph on page 22 to solve the puzzle.

A Beautiful Fiber Crossword Puzzle

Across

2 A silkworm creates this to make its cocoon
3 Silkworms are kept in this type of environment on silk farms
4 Silk garments resist this
5 Where silk production takes place
7 Bright in appearance

Down

1 Another word for cloth
3 Silk fabrics can be dyed in a variety of these
4 An animal that makes silk
5 Another word for thread
6 A type of fiber

Total Problems: Total Correct: Score:

Name _____   **Eat Your Veggies!**

Read the passage and answer the questions. Circle the letter beside the correct answer.

Eat Your Veggies!

Vegetables are an important source of nutrition. There are many different kinds of vegetables, and it is best to eat a variety with your meals each day. There are different types of vegetables available to us. Some are easily grown in your own backyard. Vegetables like lettuce, cabbage, spinach, parsley, and asparagus are important because of their leaves and the important vitamins and minerals they contribute to a healthy diet. Other vegetables like potatoes, carrots, onions, beets, and turnips grow underground and are the root of the plant. Did you realize you were eating a root the last time you ate a carrot?

When you eat vegetables, you give your body necessary vitamins, like A and C, as well as minerals like calcium and iron. Vegetables do not have a lot of calories, and they don't provide as much energy as other foods do. But, they are helpful in other ways. Beans and peas provide protein when eaten with foods like rice and whole grains. Protein is needed for building muscle and strength.

Vegetables are interesting foods. Some are delicious if eaten raw, while others are better if they are cooked. They come in many different colors, shapes, and sizes. Eating vegetables that are new to you can be a tasty and healthy thing to do!

1. What part of the plant is a carrot?
    A. the stem
    B. the root
    C. the leaf
    D. the flower

2. Why is it important to eat a variety of vegetables?
    A. Some vegetables are better than others.
    B. They are hard to grow.
    C. Vegetables give your body vitamins and minerals.
    D. You would get bored if you ate the same vegetables all the time.

3. Which of the following are leafy green vegetables?
    A. lettuce, cabbage, and spinach
    B. spinach, onions, and parsley
    C. asparagus, lettuce, and potatoes
    D. tomatoes, lettuce, and spinach

24   Total Problems: _____   Total Correct: _____   Score: _____

© Carson-Dellosa CD-2203

Refer to the passage on page 24 to solve the puzzle.

Eat Your Veggies! Crossword Puzzle

Across

2 Needed to build muscle and strength
4 Another word for an assortment
7 Some vegetables grow here
9 Another word for not cooked
10 Spinach, lettuce, and cabbage are important because of these

Down

1 This is an important source of nutrition
3 Vegetables contain _____ and minerals
5 Vegetables do not have a lot of these
6 Some examples of these are iron and calcium
8 Carrots, beets, and turnips are the _____ of the plant

Total Problems:	Total Correct:	Score:

Read the passage and answer the questions on the following page.

Tennis, Anyone?

The game of tennis has been in existence for many years. It is played on a large court with rackets and balls. The players hit the ball back and forth over a net that is in the middle of the court. If two people play tennis against each other, it is called "singles." If four people play at one time, it is called "doubles."

The net in the middle of the court is three feet high. There are different types of outdoor tennis courts. Grass, asphalt, and clay courts are the most common types. Indoor courts are sometimes made of wood or canvas coverings.

The first player to get four points wins the game. Points are counted in a some-what unusual way. The first point is called 15. The second is 30, and the third is 40. Oddly, the score of zero is called "love" in tennis. The last point is the "game point." It does not have a number. If two players reach 40 at the same time, the first player to get the next two points will win the game. In a large tennis tournament, the players must play a lot of games to win the tournament.

A "set" has been won when a player has won at least six games. Usually, a set has more than six games in it. A match is won when a player wins at least two sets. If the player wins the first two sets, a third set does not have to be played.

Tennis is a very active game that can be played with great skill and athletic ability. Players must practice if they expect to excel at this game. It is possible to become a very good tennis player at a young age. Tennis has a rich history and is full of great men and women players. As with any sport, it is important to have a good attitude toward the other players in the game.

Name _____

Answer the questions. Write a "T" in the blank next to each statement below that is true. Write an "F" if the statement is false.

1. _____ Tennis is played on a court.

2. _____ Tennis is not played indoors.

3. _____ The net is located on the side of the court.

4. _____ There are only two players in a singles game of tennis.

5. _____ A player has to get four points to win a game.

6. _____ A set consists of at least six games.

7. _____ Men and women can be good tennis players.

Write your answer to question #8 on the lines provided below.

8. Explain why you think it is important to keep a good attitude toward the other players in any sport.

_____

_____

_____

_____

_____

_____

_____

_____

Total Problems: Total Correct: Score: **27**

Name _____

Read the passage and answer the questions on the following page.

Hello, Mr. Bell

Alexander Graham Bell was a teacher from Scotland who came to the United States to live and work. He taught in Boston, Massachusetts, at a school for deaf children. At home in the evenings he worked on his hobby of making things to help his students. One day in June he was busily working with his partner, Thomas A. Watson, when he accidentally discovered the telephone.

Mr. Bell and Mr. Watson were trying to find a way to make a telegraph that could transmit several messages at one time across a single wire. While Mr. Bell was working in another room, Mr. Watson snapped one of the wooden reeds on the telegraph to loosen it. This caused a change in the electric currents flowing across the wire and actually carried sound. Mr. Bell was so excited. He actually heard Mr. Watson in the other room talking about breaking the reed! Mr. Watson was worried that he had disconnected the telegraph.

Mr. Bell quickly went to find his partner in the other room and tell him what had happened. Both men were fascinated by what they had accomplished. Mr. Bell took his invention to the United States Patent Office to officially register it as his invention. Soon it became known that a long-distance speaking device was available. A doctor in Boston wanted a telephone so that he could speak to his wife at home while he was at his office three miles away. This was the first long-distance telephone installed for a customer.

The telephone quickly became popular. Mr. Bell realized there was a need to continue working on the invention to make it even better. This would make communication between people in different buildings possible. Eventually people would be able to talk to others in different cities.

Today we are able to use the telephone to talk to people in different countries and send faxes and electronic mail messages all because of the original discovery of Alexander Graham Bell on June 2, 1875. We consider the telephone a very important invention, and we rely on it every day.

Answer the questions. Circle the letter beside the correct answer. Or, write the answer on the lines provided.

1. What was Mr. Bell's hobby?
    A. making telephones
    B. making telegraphs
    C. making things for deaf students
    D. making patents

2. Where was Alexander Graham Bell from?
    A. Massachusetts
    B. Maine
    C. England
    D. Scotland

3. What was unusual about the invention of the telephone?
    A. It was invented by two men working together.
    B. The inventor was a deaf man.
    C. The invention was supposed to be a larger telegraph.
    D. It was invented in the United States instead of another country.

4. Explain why early customers might have wanted telephones.

    _____

    _____

    _____

    _____

    _____

5. How is the telephone helpful to us today?

    _____

    _____

    _____

    _____

    _____

Total Problems:	Total Correct:	Score:

Read the passage and answer the questions on the following page.

Zachary Taylor

Zachary Taylor was the twelfth president of the United States. He was born in Barboursville, Virginia, in 1784. He was the son of Richard and Sarah Taylor. Zachary's father was a plantation owner. As a young boy, Zachary helped his father with the family's farm. He had five brothers and three sisters.

Zachary grew up in the midst of Indian warfare in the 1800s. He did not attend school because there were no schools during that time. He had tutors, and he also learned many lessons by working with his father on the farm. His family was one of the largest slave owners in the South, and later as president of the United States, he opposed freeing the slaves.

Military service was where Zachary Taylor was most effective. He led armies to victory several times in his career. His soldiers nicknamed him "old rough and ready" because he was very skilled at leading troops into battle. He once received a war bonus of six thousand acres of land. He later settled on some of it in Kentucky .

In 1810, Mr. Taylor married a woman named Margaret Smith. They later had a son and five daughters. Zachary Taylor was president for only sixteen months. He became ill in July of 1850 and soon died. His incomplete term was completed by his vice president, Millard Fillmore. During Mr. Taylor's presidency, the United States experienced the Gold Rush of 1849. In addition, the Overland Mail Service and the Office of the Interior were created during this time.

Answer the questions. Circle the letter beside the correct answer. Or, write the answer on the lines provided.

1. Zachary Taylor was the _____ U.S. president.
   A. eleventh   B. fourteenth
   C. twelfth   D. second

2. Where did Zachary Taylor get an education?
   A. in school   B. from books
   C. at college   D. at home, from tutors

3. Who were Zachary Taylor's parents?
   A. Margaret and John
   B. Richard and Sarah
   C. Sarah and Thomas
   D. Millard and Elizabeth

4. What is another word for "plantation"?
   A. farm
   B. cabin
   C. town
   D. garden

5. How long did Taylor serve as United States president?
   A. one year, three months
   B. two years
   C. one year, six months
   D. one year, four months

6. Who was Millard Fillmore?
   A. the vice president
   B. the secretary
   C. a soldier in the army
   D. Zachary's father

7. Do you think Zachary Taylor was a good president? Explain why or why not.

   _____

   _____

   _____

   _____

Name _____

Read the passage and answer the questions on the following page.

Dolly and Brittany

Dolly and Brittany were waiting in the kitchen for their owners, Mr. and Mrs. Moore, to come home when a loud thunderstorm started. The walls of the house seemed to shake with each clap of thunder. This scared the puppies, and they began to whine. The pet gate was wedged in the doorway of the kitchen to keep them from running through the house. Dolly tried several times to push it over. She wasn't strong enough to do that, so she tried biting the wooden frame of the gate.

In the meantime, Brittany was walking back and forth across the kitchen floor. She was very worried and restless. Suddenly, she heard a loud noise and ran to see what it was. Dolly had chewed the pet gate, causing the wooden bar to break and fall out of the doorway. They were free! Both dogs began to bark happily as they scampered down the hall to look for Mr. and Mrs. Moore. They quickly searched all of the bedrooms, but they found no one.

Disappointed, the two dogs went into the den and jumped on the sofa. That's when Dolly noticed a bowl of nuts on the table. She climbed over the edge of the sofa and began eating them out of the bowl. Brittany saw what Dolly was doing and went over to see if any nuts were left. Instead, Brittany found another bowl on the table. It had pretzels! Both dogs ate until the snacks were gone.

Just as they were about to settle down, another clap of thunder shook the house. The rain continued to pummel the house with great force. This upset Dolly and Brittany very much so they began to dig furiously on the sofa. Dolly dug so hard and fast the stuffing began to come out of the cushion. They tried to settle down again, but more noises continued to disturb them. The telephone rang, the clock in the hall chimed, and cars drove down the street.

Just then, the front door opened. It was Mr. and Mrs. Moore! Mr. Moore let his wife inside while he shook his umbrella on the porch. Brittany, trying to get to the door, jumped off the sofa. Her feet bumped the table so hard that the lamp and bowls came crashing to the floor. Mrs. Moore heard the loud noise and saw Brittany running to greet her.

Mr. Moore looked at the dogs and said, "Just what have you been up to lately?" The dogs just sat there, trying to look as cute as possible. Mr. and Mrs. Moore hung up their wet coats and umbrella and started toward the den. They had no idea what they were about to find!

Answer the questions. Write the answers on the lines provided.

1. What is this story about?

   _____

   _____

   _____

2. Who are the characters in this story?

   _____

   _____

3. What is the setting for this story?

   _____

   _____

4. What is the problem in this story?

   _____

   _____

   _____

   _____

5. Why are the people in the story going to be surprised?

   _____

   _____

   _____

   _____

Read the passage and answer the questions on the following page.

Aunt Mary's Baby

My Aunt Mary is going to have a baby soon. I am so excited because I live down the street from her, and I can visit the baby whenever I want. My mom is Aunt Mary's sister. Mom says it is going to be great having a new little cousin. I have two older brothers, Lee and Ryan. They are huge baseball fans. I am the only girl, and I like sports, too. My name is Joanna, and I like being the youngest in my family.

Aunt Mary and Uncle Kyle plan to name their baby Ethan if it is a boy and Nicole if it is a girl. I like those names. I hope it is a girl. I went to Aunt Mary's house almost every day for about three weeks this summer. I was helping her get the baby's room ready. I helped put the clothes in the drawers, hang pictures on the walls, and put sheets and blankets in the crib. I also put all of the stuffed animals on a bookshelf in the baby's room for the baby to see when he or she is awake. Aunt Mary said a baby's room is sometimes called a nursery. This nursery is certainly the cutest I have ever seen.

When the baby gets home, he or she will sleep a lot. Aunt Mary and Uncle Kyle will have to feed the baby often and change diapers, too. Their dog Coco may become jealous of the baby. Coco has never seen a baby before. I think Coco will like the baby. When the baby can play and walk, Coco will have lots of fun!

I sometimes feel like time is going by so slowly, and the baby will never arrive. But, Mom tells me that it will be here before we know it. I will go to Aunt Mary's house every day so the baby will know who I am. It will be so much fun!

Name _____

Answer the questions. Circle the letter beside the correct answer. Or, write the answer on the lines provided.

1. Who is having a baby?
   A. Nicole   B. Mom
   C. Mary   D. Coco

2. This story is being told by:
   A. a young girl   B. a mother
   C. a boy   D. a baby

3. Why did Joanna visit Aunt Mary during the summer?
   A. She watched the baby for her aunt.
   B. She helped decorate the baby's room.
   C. She took care of the dog.
   D. She looked for her brothers.

4. If the baby is a boy, what will they name it?
   A. Lee   B. John
   C. Ethan   D. Ryan

5. Why might the dog become jealous of the baby?
   A. It has never seen a baby.
   B. Babies do not like dogs.
   C. The dog is scared of it.
   D. There was not a dog in this story.

6. What did the story mention that new babies often do?
   A. cry
   B. eat
   C. sleep
   D. play

7. Describe how you think the author feels about having a new baby cousin.

   _____

   _____

   _____

   _____

   _____

Total Problems: Total Correct: Score:

Read the poem and answer the questions. Circle the letter beside the correct answer.

July

I'll jump into the swimming pool,
I hope to find it comfortably cool.
The sun is hot and the air is dry,
Fluffy, white clouds float on by.
Summer is so much fun for me,
This is exactly how I like to be.
Schedules and homework are gone away,
I laugh and play with friends each day.
Vacations end but memories last,
The summer passes way too fast.

1. What is the main idea of this poem?
   A. The author likes to swim.
   B. You see many kinds of clouds in the summer.
   C. The author enjoys summer for many reasons.
   D. Funny things happen at a pool.

2. Why does the poem say that homework has gone away?
   A. It is summer, and there is no school or homework.
   B. He is dreaming that there will not be any homework.
   C. He lost his homework and hopes the teacher will not know.
   D. Homework is too hard.

3. What does the poem say will last after summer is over?
   A. clouds   B. memories
   C. vacations   D. friends

4. How many lines does the poem have?
   A. 8   B. 7
   C. 10   D. 12

5. In this poem every _____ lines rhyme.
   A. 4   B. 2
   C. 6   D. 8

6. The author of this poem is most likely what age?
   A. 22   B. 10   C. 2   D. 30

36

Total Problems:	Total Correct:	Score:

Refer to the poem on page 36 to solve the puzzle.

July Crossword Puzzle

Across

2 If you think something is funny, you might do this
6 _____ and homework are gone away
9 Something you swim in
10 The season this poem is about

Down

1 Another word for times spent away from school
3 An assignment to be done after school
4 Vacations end but _____ last
5 Fluffy, white objects in the sky
7 The opposite of warm
8 Where you find clouds

Total Problems:	Total Correct:	Score:

Name _____

Read the passage and answer the questions on the following page.

Jacques Cousteau

A pioneer is a person who does something new before anyone else. He or she may travel to a new place or discover something no one else has discovered. We often read about the brave pioneers of our country and the explorers who discovered how huge the new land of America was. However, there is another world we often forget. It is the ocean. Under the waves lies a vast region of sea life and unusually shaped places. There are pioneers of underwater places, too!

A famous man named Jacques Cousteau was a pioneer of the underwater world. He was French, and he made some wonderful and helpful discoveries under the sea. He swam very well and took pictures of underwater life. Many people had never seen this before, so it was very exciting. Jacques Cousteau was also a great writer. He often wrote about his diving experiences. He even made a movie about what he had learned. The movie, *The Silent World*, won an Academy Award.

Exploring the ocean was a big thrill for Jacques Cousteau. But, he knew it would be easier to explore if he could hold his breath longer, or invent a way to take extra oxygen with him. This desire caused him to invent the Aqua-Lung™, or S.C.U.B.A. (self-contained underwater breathing apparatus). This is a large tank filled with oxygen that divers wear when they explore the underwater world. The Aqua-Lung™ made diving much easier. Divers could stay under the water longer and get more information on their trips.

Jacques Cousteau continued to dive until he reached the age of seventy-five. He was very intelligent and had so much experience that younger dive crews would ask him to ride with them during an exploration. His experience and knowledge was a valuable aid to divers and scientists as they learned about the underwater world.

Answer the questions. Circle the letter beside the correct answer.

1. What did Jacques Cousteau do?
    A.   He explored America.
    B.   He explored the ocean.
    C.   He invented boats.
    D.   He liked to fish.

2. Where was Jacques Cousteau from?
    A.   England
    B.   America
    C.   France
    D.   Italy

3. What diving tool did he invent?
    A.   the bathing suit
    B.   the S.C.U.B.A. tank
    C.   the camera
    D.   the Academy Award

4. According to the passage, what other talent did Jacques Cousteau have?
    A.   singing
    B.   writing
    C.   cooking
    D.   flying

5. According to the passage, what is a pioneer?
    A.   Someone who explores oceans.
    B.   A person who travels to a new place first or discovers something new.
    C.   People who want to move to a new house.
    D.   Divers who want to take pictures under water.

6. Why did younger divers want Mr. Cousteau to go on trips with them?
    A.   They needed him to drive the boat.
    B.   They needed to use his S.C.U.B.A. equipment.
    C.   They knew he could make the trip into a movie.
    D.   He knew a lot about the sea and diving.

7. What was the name of the movie Jacques Cousteau made?
    A.   *The Water World*   B.   *The Best Ocean*
    C.   *The Silent World*   D.   *The Fish and Me*

Total Problems:	Total Correct:	Score:

39

Name _____

Read the paragraph and answer the questions. Circle the letter beside the correct answer.

Hawaii

Hawaii is the only U.S. state that does not lie on the mainland of North America. It is made up entirely of islands in the Pacific Ocean. It is also the southernmost state in the United States. The primary religion of Hawaii is Roman Catholic. Some Asian families of Hawaii are worshipers of the Buddhist religion. Farming is a big business on the islands. The soil is very fertile for planting various crops. The climate is warm year-round which makes a longer growing season possible. Hawaii also has a large tourist industry. It is a popular destination for people who like the beach and history. Hawaii was first inhabited by the Polynesians. In later years, other races and nationalities have moved to the islands. The beautiful flowers and Hawaiian dancers are notable features of the state. Most people fly to the Hawaiian islands from the United States and other places. Boats are also often used.

1. Hawaii is made of _____.
   A. volcanoes
   C. mountains
   B. islands
   D. oceans

2. Hawaii is located in the _____ Ocean.
   A. Indian
   B. Polynesian
   C. Pacific
   D. Atlantic

3. What are two large industries in Hawaii?
   A. tourism and farming
   B. farming and fishing
   C. boating and fishing
   D. trading and travel

4. A reasonable explanation for the beautiful flowers in Hawaii is:
   A. Many scientists live there and study the way to grow flowers all year.
   B. The fertile soil and the warm, year-round temperatures provide ideal conditions.
   C. The tourist industry provides enough money for the state to buy nice flowers.
   D. Many residents of Hawaii have their own gardens.

5. According to the paragraph, why would people be interested in visiting Hawaii?
   A. beautiful beaches, history, and warm climate
   B. beautiful churches, farming, and nice hotels
   C. excellent schools, good economy, and good location
   D. good restaurants, excellent jobs, and good pay

Total Problems: _____   Total Correct: _____   Score: _____

Name _____

Read the passage and answer the questions. Write a "T" in the blank next to each statement below that is true. Write an "F" if the statement is false.

Portugal

I am visiting a new place this summer with my grandparents. It is Lisbon, Portugal. Portugal is small compared to the United States. In fact, it is only a little larger than the whole state of Maine. The people here speak Portuguese, which is a lot like Spanish. Spain is very close to Portugal, so there are some things in Portugal that are like Spain.

Some people who live here fish, and others help with trading goods to other countries. Fishing and bringing in fresh seafood are big jobs in Portugal. Some families have farms and grow things to sell. There are also famous wine makers in the country, and fruits are grown here, too. We have eaten delicious fruit desserts every night after dinner. We've eaten a lot of seafood here, too.

I have enjoyed my visit to Portugal. I can't wait to get back to the United States and tell my friends about the things we have seen. I hope we can get our pictures developed quickly. When I return to school, I might do a report on Portugal for my teacher. I will have a lot to tell and pictures to go with it! This has been a really fun vacation.

1. _____ The fishing industry is very important in Portugal.

2. _____ Spanish is somewhat like Portuguese.

3. _____ Many people in Portugal work for large banks.

4. _____ The person telling this story is most likely a child.

5. _____ The characters in this story are from Spain.

6. _____ Portugal is smaller than Maine.

7. _____ Fruits are grown in Portugal.

Total Problems: Total Correct: Score:

Read the passage and answer the questions on the following page.

Basketball Camp

My friend Jake and I love to play basketball. This fall we are going to go to a basketball camp on Saturdays. It is going to last all day. We are very excited. I have a basketball hoop in my driveway at home. Jake comes over every day after school, and we play together. I am better at layups than him. He is taller than I am, so his jump shot is better than mine. We have other interests in common, too, but basketball is our favorite. My name is Blake. My dad calls us the "basketball akes" because both of our names end with the letters "a", "k", and "e." He thinks he is so funny!

When we get to camp, the leaders will divide us into groups. I guess that is like being on teams. We will go to different courts both in the gymnasium and outside to practice drills and game strategies. I hope that Jake and I will be in the same group. I want to learn how to be a better basketball player.

After several Saturdays, we are going to play a game with other groups. The winners of those groups will then play each other. This is like a tournament. The last winning team is the champion! I know that it would be a lot of fun to win, but learning about the game will be fun for me. All of the kids were told that at the end of the camp a famous basketball player is going to come and meet us. No one knows who it is. Jake and I hope it is Michael Jordan. We think he is the best basketball player of all time! This is going to be a great camp. I can't wait until Saturday gets here. I am ready to go! I know Jake is, too.

Answer the questions below. Circle the letter beside the correct answer. Or, write the answer on the lines provided.

1. When are the boys going to basketball camp?
   - A. next summer
   - C. after school
   - B. on Saturdays
   - D. next year

2. What does Blake hope to learn at camp?
   - A. how to get along with others
   - C. how to play better basketball
   - B. how to play on a good team
   - D. how to coach basketball

3. Where will the groups practice their game strategies?
   - A. outside
   - C. outside and inside
   - B. inside
   - D. at home

4. What skill is Jake better at than Blake?
   - A. jump shots
   - C. layups
   - B. free throws
   - D. passing

5. What special game is going to be played at the end of the camp?
   - A. championship
   - C. scramble
   - B. tournament
   - D. match

6. Who is going to visit the kids at the camp?
   - A. a famous basketball player
   - C. no one
   - B. their parents
   - D. their teachers

7. On the lines below write a paragraph about a sport you like or have seen being played. Use descriptive words to make your paragraph interesting.

   _____

   _____

   _____

   _____

   _____

   _____

   _____

   _____

Name _____

Read the passage and answer the questions on the following page.

House Hunting

Melanie Miller and her parents flew into Chicago last night. The Millers are moving because Melanie's father received a job promotion. This is exciting and a little scary because Melanie doesn't know anyone in the new place. After breakfast today, the Miller family will begin their search for a new house.

Mr. Miller has to work in the city, but Mrs. Miller hopes to find a house in the suburbs. Melanie wants to find a neighborhood that has a lot of kids. She is even hoping there is a community swimming pool nearby. The Miller's old neighborhood in Atlanta, Georgia, had the best pool, and Melanie knew every kid on her street. Mrs. Miller tried to reassure her daughter that the process of making friends would take awhile. They had lived at their old house for nine years, so it was no surprise that Melanie felt so comfortable there and knew so many people.

The family finished their breakfast in the hotel restaurant and went to the lobby to meet their real estate agent. Mrs. Jenkins told the Millers she was very excited to see them. She was anxious to get started because there were several houses she wanted to show them.

The first one was a large, red brick house with huge bedrooms and lots of closets. The kitchen was big and fancy. Mrs. Miller was not sure she needed a kitchen that big. The next house they looked at was also large and had several rooms, a basement, and a big backyard. The third house had two fireplaces and a living room that was large enough to hold three sofas! Melanie had never seen a house that big before. The ceilings were really high, and the rooms seemed to have an echo. The last house they saw also had a basement, and the bedrooms all had private bathrooms. Melanie liked the idea of having a basement. It would be one more room for her books and games. It was very big, and her father said the house even had enough room for him to have a small office.

Melanie liked all of the houses Mrs. Jenkins showed her family. Now it was up to her parents to talk it over and decide where the family should live. Finally, they decided on the second house they had seen. It was the one with a basement and a huge backyard. Mr. and Mrs. Miller finished talking to Mrs. Jenkins, and they signed the contract before they left. When they got back to the hotel, Mrs. Miller suggested that they go play miniature golf. Melanie and her father liked that idea, so they went.

Answer the questions. Circle the letter beside the correct answer.

1. Why is the Miller family moving to a new house?
    A.   Mr. Miller has a new job in a different town.
    B.   Mrs. Miller wanted to move to the suburbs.
    C.   Their old house was too small for them.
    D.   They didn't have a swimming pool.

2. How long did the Millers live in Atlanta, Georgia?
    A.   five years
    B.   two years
    C.   eight years
    D.   nine years

3. Where did the Miller family see Mrs. Jenkins?
    A.   Atlanta
    B.   Chicago
    C.   Boston
    D.   New York

4. How many houses did the Millers see on their house-hunting tour?
    A.   four
    B.   three
    C.   five
    D.   one

5. Why did Melanie like the idea of having a house with a basement?
    A.   She could have a special place to play.
    B.   It made the house seem larger.
    C.   Her father needed an office.
    D.   Houses with basements always have larger yards.

6. Which house did the family decide to buy?
    A.   the first one
    B.   the second one
    C.   the fifth one
    D.   the fourth one

Total Problems:	Total Correct:	Score:

Name _____

Read the passage and answer the questions on the following page.

Another Use for Seeds

Karsen got off the school bus still puzzled by her teacher's art assignment. Just hours ago she was sitting in Mrs. Pennington's art class listening to her teacher explain the next assignment. The teacher explained that she wanted each student to "artfully present" his or her own house. Karsen immediately thought of her collection of markers, crayons, colored pencils, and watercolors. She could make a very artful presentation with the huge range of colors she had to choose from. She was sure this project would be a breeze. However, Mrs. Pennington then said that no crayons, paints, or markers could be used. Karsen and her classmates were stunned! This would be impossible. How could they draw without those materials?

Several students asked questions, but Mrs. Pennington simply answered that everyone should use their imagination. Class ended and it was time to go to lunch. Karsen, Leah, and Sonya sat together at lunch chatting about the strange art assignment. Leah said she was going to ask her father for help since he was an architect. Leah said her grandmother was always doing crafts, so she was planning to ask her.

When Karsen arrived home, her little brother Dylan had to go to his soccer game. Karsen didn't want to go but her mother encouraged her to come with them because her father was going to meet them at the game. While Dylan played, Karsen headed to the concession stand to get a snack. Karsen got a drink and a package of sunflower seeds and went back to join her mother. Soon her dad arrived, and they watched the game and chatted about school. Karsen told her parents about the weird art assignment and asked for suggestions. Her father agreed to help her after the game.

Still bothered about not having an idea, Karsen began playing with her empty sunflower seed shells. She began placing them in rows and circles on the seat beside her. She quickly noticed that the seeds could create a picture. And, seeds come in different colors. She could make a mosaic using seeds! Karsen was excited about her discovery and began planning her project. She would use pumpkin seeds for the white painted wood on their house and corn seeds for the yellow shutters. Her mind was racing with great ideas.

This was an original idea. Now the project would be fun to do. At home that evening Karsen's father came up to her room to help her with the project as he had promised. Karsen told him her idea and said that he could help her glue the seeds to the paper. Karsen got all of the paper and materials she would need for the project, and they began working.

Answer the questions. Circle the letter beside the correct answer.

1. What did Karsen have to create for art class?
    A.   a painting of her pet
    B.   a picture of her house
    C.   a drawing of her family
    D.   a model of her school

2. Why did Mrs. Pennington not want the students to use the usual art supplies?
    A.   She wanted them to use recycled material.
    B.   She didn't have many of the art supplies.
    C.   She wanted the students to use their imaginations.
    D.   She was trying to follow the rules for the art contest.

3. How did Karsen come up with the idea of using seeds in the picture?
    A.   Her father told her to use them.
    B.   Her friends were using seeds, so she decided to do that also.
    C.   She got the idea from playing with her empty sunflower seeds.
    D.   She saw the idea on television.

4. Why did Karsen go to the soccer game?
    A.   She was very interested in the sport.
    B.   Her dad was going to be there.
    C.   Her brother had a game.
    D.   She wanted sunflower seeds.

5. According to the context clues, the word "mosaic" most likely means:
    A.   likeness
    B.   made of seeds
    C.   colorful
    D.   picture or design

Name _____

Holiday Shopping

Read the passage and answer the questions. Circle the letter beside the correct answer.

Holiday Shopping

Katie and Lisa love to go holiday shopping with their mothers. They had been saving their baby-sitting money so that they wouldn't have to ask their parents for spending money this year. The girls were more excited than ever! They were planning to go the day after Thanksgiving and be there in the morning when the mall opened. That way they would get to the stores while the merchandise was still folded and ready for shoppers. Katie's favorite stores are specialty clothing stores with cool clothes. Lisa prefers the department stores where there are clothes, jewelry, and makeup. The girls wanted to go to as many stores as possible this year. This was going to be a great shopping trip.

Katie called Lisa that morning, and the girls chatted eagerly about their plan for the day. The girls decided to meet at Lisa's house and ride with their mothers to the mall. Lunch would be at the food court. After shopping, they would return to Lisa's house and order a pizza.

Lisa's mom drove everyone to the mall and parked near the department store entrance. Everyone decided to meet at the water fountain in the center of the mall at twelve-thirty to eat lunch and again at four-thirty to return home. Katie and Lisa would be on their own for shopping. Lisa wanted to find a gift for her grandmother and her little brother Joey. Katie wanted to look for gifts for her father and her sister Michelle.

1. Who are the main characters in this story?
   A. Kate and Lisa
   B. Katie and Lisa
   C. Kelly and her mom
   D. Lisa and Katie's parents

2. When did the girls go on their shopping trip?
   A. after Thanksgiving
   B. after the holidays
   C. summer
   D. spring

3. Where did the girls go shopping?
   A. the mall
   B. the shopping center
   C. the music store
   D. the computer place

4. Why was this shopping trip different than ones in the past?
   A. The girls were going to be allowed to eat lunch by the fountain.
   B. The girls were allowed to stay all day at the mall.
   C. The girls had their own money to spend.
   D. The girls went without their mothers.

48

Total Problems: ____   Total Correct: ____   Score: ____

© Carson-Dellosa CD-2203

Name _____

Read the passage and answer the questions. Write the answers on the lines provided.

Mr. FBI

When you think of the FBI, visions of uniformed sharp shooters probably come to mind. While they are a vital part of the Federal Bureau of Investigation, they are just one part. The bureau, commonly known by its initials, is a government organization that focuses on eliminating organized crime and dealing with public enemies. The bureau was staffed with untrained men in its beginning. That changed in 1924, when a man named J. Edgar Hoover took over the top-ranked position. He replaced the less-skilled employees with lawyers and accountants.

As a lawyer himself, Mr. Hoover knew how valuable legal knowledge was in fighting crime. He had a vision for the United States. He wanted a strong agency to tackle crime and help local police precincts in their battles against crime. He got just that. Mr. Hoover led the FBI from 1924 to 1972. During that time, he developed ways to identify criminals and solve even the toughest cases. He helped develop ways to use human fingerprints to identify criminals. He began the huge task of getting police stations to become more organized. He also developed ways to use technology and laboratories to solve unusual crimes.

1. According to the story, who is credited with building up the FBI?

   _____

2. What were some of the changes he brought to the agency?

   _____

   _____

   _____

3. What did he want the local polices stations to do?

   _____

4. How long was Hoover in charge of the government agency?

   _____

5. What profession did Mr. Hoover have originally?

   _____

Read the passage and answer the questions. Circle the letter beside the correct answer. Or, write the answer on the lines provided.

Accidental Inventions

Inventions sometimes happen by mistake. For instance, an inventor might have an idea for a new device. As it is being developed, the inventor might realize that there could be another use for the tool. It may be a completely different use than he or she first imagined. Creating a new tool, machine, or toy can be a long or short process. Of course, more complex inventions normally will take a longer time to create.

Once an invention is designed and there is a valid purpose for it, the inventor might show it to other people to determine if it could be manufactured and sold to the public. That is how many inventions become common household products. Imagine what your life would be like without a vacuum cleaner, a telephone, or a lamp! We use so many inventions each day that we often forget or overlook their value to us.

Once the item has been created, the inventor may want to protect the idea and the invention by getting a patent. This is a legal way of saying that the idea and invention belong to the inventor.

1. Why are some inventions created by accident?

    _____

    _____

2. A person who invents things is called a(n) _____.
    A. genius   B. inventor
    C. invention   D. scientist

3. Name several inventions you use in your home.

    _____

    _____

4. How long should it take to invent something?
    A. about two months   B. about one year
    C. no specific time limit   D. only a few weeks

5. Why is it a good idea to get a patent for an invention?
    A. You can show it to your friends.   B. It is not expensive.
    C. It will protect your idea.   D. It will be easier to sell your idea.

Total Problems: _____   Total Correct: _____   Score: _____

Name _____

Read the poem and answer the questions. Circle the letter beside the correct answer. Or, write the answer on the lines provided.

Rain

The water feels fresh and clean on my face;
It makes me slow to a careful pace.
The puddles surprise my feet as I walk;
I like how the noises cover the talk.
I hold my umbrella and walk to the door,
Then place my galoshes on the floor.
It feels all cozy and warm inside;
I sit by the fire and pretend to hide.
From the misty outdoors to the warm pleasures here,
The reasons I'm home are perfectly clear.

1. What does the author mean by the phrase "makes me slow to a careful pace"?
   A. It is difficult to walk in the rain, so the author is careful.
   B. The author likes walking in the rain and getting wet.
   C. The author is really taking a shower.
   D. Rain always makes people walk much slower than normal.

2. What does the author mean by the phrase "the puddles surprise my feet as I walk"?
   A. The author's feet don't know that it is raining.
   B. The author's feet suddenly get wet, which is like a surprise.
   C. The author's feet are tricked by the puddles of water on the ground.
   D. The author accidentally fell into a puddle of water.

3. How do you think the author feels at home?
   A. unhappy
   B. pleased
   C. lonely
   D. tired

4. On the lines below describe an experience you've had in the rain.

   _____

   _____

   _____

   _____

Total Problems: Total Correct: Score:

Read the passage and answer the questions. Circle the letter beside the correct answer.

Leave It to the Leaves

Leaves are the food-producing part of plants. They act as little "factories" for making food for the plant. Most leaves are flat and green. The leaf contains a green chemical called chlorophyll, which is necessary in the process of making food. This food-making process is called photosynthesis. In this process, the chlorophyll in the leaf reacts when sunlight contacts it. The wide, flat leaf makes it easy for sunlight to shine on the leaf blade. Carbon dioxide combines with the water in this process, and ultimately, food is made for the plant.

Once the food is made in the leaves, the plant may store the food in the stem, roots, fruit, or seeds. Leaves vary in shape and size. Some plants have many leaves, while others have only a few. Grass is an example of a very common, long narrow leaf. A blade of grass is a leaf. Inside each leaf is a system of tiny veins which transport the plant's nutrients. Grass blades have parallel veins. Some leaves have veins that branch out and form a wide or oval leaf blade. Leaves are vital to the life of every plant.

1. How are leaves like factories?
    - A. They make new plants.
    - B. They make flowers.
    - C. They make the plant's food.
    - D. They make fruits.

2. What is the green chemical in leaves that is necessary for making food?
    - A. chloroplasts
    - B. chlorophyll
    - C. veins
    - D. fruit

3. Where might a plant store food?
    - A. stem, roots, soil, leaves
    - B. stem, roots, fruit, seeds
    - C. bud, stem, branches, flower
    - D. stem, leaf, bark, petal

4. Long, narrow leaves have what type of vein arrangement?
    - A. parallel
    - B. wide
    - C. narrow
    - D. round

5. What does a leaf need to make food for a plant?
    - A. carbon dioxide, sunlight, water, and grass
    - B. carbon dioxide, water, sunlight, chlorophyll
    - C. carbon dioxide, roots, leaves, sunlight
    - D. carbon dioxide, stems, veins, sunlight

Total Problems:	Total Correct:	Score:

Refer to the passage on page 52 to solve the puzzle.

Leave It to the Leaves Crossword Puzzle

Across

2 _____ dioxide and water help make plant food
3 The food-producing part of a plant
4 A common leaf color
6 The plant process of making food
9 Blades of grass have this type of vein arrangement

Down

1 Important substances for proper growth, from the base word "nourish"
2 A green substance used in photosynthesis
5 Liquid necessary for life
7 The tall supporting part of a plant
8 Light from the sun

Total Problems:	Total Correct:	Score:

Read the passage and answer the questions on the following page.

Nancy's Office

Nancy is ten years old. Her bedroom is upstairs in her family's house. Nancy loves her room, but it is full of stuff. Her mom is always telling her to straighten it up and make it look neater. She can usually tidy up enough to make her mom happy, but her room is never really organized. Nancy wanted to be organized. She just didn't know how. She knew it would be easier to find things if everything had a place. This would be a good project for her.

Nancy went to her father's office one day after school and waited in the lobby for him to take her home. Her father was in a meeting, so she had several minutes to wait. She began talking with Cheryl, a woman who worked with her dad. Cheryl had a very neat desk with drawers on the side and file cabinets behind her. When she received phone calls each day, she kept the messages in a neat stack. Whenever she needed a paper, she could find it in a file. Cheryl's office was very organized!

Nancy noticed everything Cheryl did. She asked Cheryl a lot of questions about her office and how she set up everything. Cheryl explained how she filed papers, kept supplies in drawers, and threw away things she no longer needed. Cheryl explained that when her desk was messy, it was often because she had not thrown away things that were old.

Nancy thought about this and made mental plans about how she could make her own "office" at home and organize all of her stuff. Nancy rode home with her father that afternoon and told him about her talk with Cheryl. She told him of her plan to organize the things in her bedroom like an office. He was glad she was excited, and he encouraged her to start this organization project immediately. He even offered to get her any supplies she might need for her new office. Nancy could hardly wait to get started. She knew her mother would be happy about her plan, too.

Answer the questions. Circle the letter beside the correct answer.

1. Where did Nancy go after school?
   A. Cheryl's house
   B. the doctor's office
   C. her father's office
   D. a meeting

2. What did Nancy and Cheryl do while waiting for Nancy's father?
   A. They planned a surprise party for Nancy's father.
   B. They ordered office supplies for Nancy's office.
   C. They talked about Cheryl's office and how she set it up.
   D. They pretended they were movie stars.

3. Which of the following was an organization tip Cheryl gave Nancy?
   A. She told her to write neatly.
   B. She told her to throw away unnecessary things.
   C. She told her to set up a good office at her house.
   D. She told her to always be on time.

4. What did Nancy tell her father on the way home?
   A. She didn't like waiting so long.
   B. She wanted to work in an office.
   C. She wanted to organize her room like an office.
   D. She wanted Cheryl to be her new baby-sitter.

5. What did Nancy's father offer to do for her?
   A. He offered to tell Nancy's mom her plan.
   B. He offered to buy her ice cream.
   C. He offered to buy her any supplies she may need.
   D. He wanted to get her a puppy if she would care for it.

6. Who will be the next person to find out about Nancy's plan?
   A. her mother
   B. her father
   C. her teacher
   D. Cheryl

Read the passage and answer the questions on the following page.

The Comforts of Home

Robin usually rode the bus home after school. She occasionally would ride with her mom or a friend's mom in a car pool. However, this particular day was different. School had ended early due to snow. Robin was excited about the snow and wanted to go outside and play in it. But first she had to get home, and that meant riding the bus.

All of the school buses were lined up in the front driveway to wait for the children. Soon each bus would depart for a careful ride to each neighborhood on its route. Robin's house was the second stop on her bus route. After all of the buses were loaded, Robin's bus slowly rolled out onto the snowy road. The children peered anxiously out of their windows at the soft blanket of snow covering the winter countryside. After the bus pulled to a stop next to her driveway, Robin gently stepped off the bus and headed for her house.

After a sluggish walk through her snow-covered yard, Robin opened the back door of her house and entered the kitchen. The lights were on, and she smelled a pot of coffee brewing. A fire was crackling in the fireplace. Calling for her father, Robin began taking off her heavy, snow-covered coat and gloves. Soon her father came into the kitchen and greeted her with a big hug. He was very happy to see her and was relieved that she had gotten home safely. The radio and television stations had announced that the weather had caused the schools to close, and traffic delays were widespread.

Robin and her father waited for the rest of their family to arrive. Her mother's car pulled into the garage minutes later, and her older sister and mother came inside. They had been able to drive safely from the local high school where her mother is a teacher and her sister is in ninth grade. Everyone was very happy to be together. Robin suggested that they make a pot of hot cocoa and watch the snow fall outside their window. Later they could build a snowman.

Answer the questions. Circle the letter beside the correct answer.

1. Why did Robin leave school early?
    A.   It was a holiday.
    B.   It was snowing.
    C.   She was sick.
    D.   She was going on a trip.

2. Who did Robin see when she arrived home?
    A.   her mother, father, and sister
    B.   her father
    C.   her mother and father
    D.   her mother and sister

3. What did Robin smell in her house when she arrived home that afternoon?
    A.   her mother's perfume and coffee
    B.   coffee and hot chocolate
    C.   coffee
    D.   pizza

4. What was the television news reporting?
    A.   traffic accidents
    B.   bad weather, traffic delays, and school closings
    C.   fires, bad weather, and traffic accidents
    D.   school accidents and bad weather

5. Why were Robin's mother and sister at the high school?
    A.   They were looking for a safe place to go in the bad weather.
    B.   They decided to meet each other there.
    C.   Her mom teaches there, and her sister is a student.
    D.   They both had a meeting to attend there.

6. What did Robin want to do after everyone got home?
    A.   watch a movie
    B.   have hot chocolate and watch the snow fall
    C.   go to bed
    D.   get a puppy

Read the passage and answer the questions on the following page.

A New Way to Communicate

When Leslie got home from school, her father greeted her at the door. He explained that he had purchased a new computer for the family and was setting it up in the kitchen. Mr. Wilson, Leslie's father, showed her how the computer would connect to the telephone line. This would allow them to send and receive messages electronically. This is called E-mail. It is just like sending a letter, but it is much faster. Mr. Wilson explained the details of electronic mail and the Internet to his daughter. She was very interested.

Leslie asked her father several questions about the new tool, and he began to show her how it worked. He began by logging onto the Internet and then their E-mail program. They had to wait a few seconds for the connection to be made, and soon they were able to begin their transmission. Mr. Wilson explained that it is necessary to have an E-mail address in order to send or receive messages this way. Since Leslie's father has E-mail at his office, she typed a note to him and sent it with one click of the mouse!

Leslie was very excited about the E-mail possibilities at her house. She wanted to call her friend Jan to see if her family had an E-mail address and a computer. Unfortunately, Leslie remembered that Jan was out of town visiting her grandparents. She would ask her when she returned. Leslie continued to dabble at the computer using the new E-mail system. This was great fun. Leslie was amazed at how fast it could send and receive messages.

Leslie's mother and brother came home later that evening. Her brother was in high school and had a lot of experience using computers. Leslie wanted to show him how to use it, but he already knew how. Although she was a little disappointed, she was still very excited about the new communication possibilities her family now had.

Name _____

Answer the questions. Circle the letter beside the correct answer.

1. Who did Leslie send a message to?
    A. her friend Jan
    B. her mom
    C. her dad
    D. her brother

2. Where was the family's computer set up?
    A. the den
    B. Leslie's bedroom
    C. the kitchen
    D. her dad's office

3. Who was Mr. Wilson?
    A. Leslie's father
    B. Leslie's teacher
    C. a neighbor
    D. Jan's father

4. What is needed to send an E-mail message?
    A. a computer, a telephone line, a mouse
    B. an e-mail address, a telephone line, a computer
    C. the Internet, a telephone, a computer
    D. a radio, a computer, a telephone

5. Why was Leslie disappointed about her brother already knowing about E-mail?
    A. He was better at it than she was.
    B. She was unable to show him something new.
    C. She was afraid he would use it all of the time.
    D. He had an E-mail address, and she did not.

6. With what did Leslie's brother have a lot of experience?
    A. computers
    B. the Internet
    C. E-mail
    D. radios

Total Problems: Total Correct: Score: **59**

© Carson-Dellosa CD-2203

Read the passage and answer the questions. Circle the letter beside the correct answer.

Dad's Surprise

School had only been out for ten days, and John and Rebecca were already bored! They had slept late and played in the yard every day. Summer camp would not start for another week, and the weather had not been great for going to the pool. They were only allowed to watch television one hour per day. They both liked to read, but they wanted to do something really exciting.

When the children's father came home from work, he said he had a surprise for the family. He received some tickets to an amusement park from a client. The park was in a nearby city, and they could go for three days. Before he had finished telling them the news, John and Rebecca were jumping up and down with excitement.

Mr. Davis, John and Rebecca's father, said the drive to the city would take about three hours. They could stay in a hotel and go to the park each day. There were rides, shows, and places to eat there. John and Rebecca could not wait! They would be there from Thursday to Saturday.

The children got their suitcases and began to pack. John and Rebecca chatted about the trip while they gathered their clothes and shoes. This was what they had been hoping for. The summer was off to a great start!

1. What were John and Rebecca packing for?
    A.   They were going on a trip.
    B.   They were going to camp.
    C.   Their family was moving.
    D.   They were going to their grandparents' house.

2. What had John and Rebecca been doing since school ended?
    A.   playing, reading, and watching movies
    B.   playing, swimming, and roller-skating
    C.   playing, sleeping late, and watching television
    D.   playing, camping, and biking

3. Where did Mr. Davis get the tickets for the amusement park?
    A.   He won them.
    B.   He got them from a client.
    C.   He got them from a friend.
    D.   He works at the park.

Total Problems: Total Correct: Score:

Refer to the passage on page 60 to solve the puzzle.

Dad's Surprise Crossword Puzzle

Across

  4   The family was going to this type of park
  8   How many days they were going to stay
  9   Where they would stay on their trip
  10   The season during which this story takes place

Down

  1   Where the children were going in a week
  2   The children's dad had a _____ for them
  3   The number between zero and two
  5   Another word for fun
  6   A bag for packing clothes in when you go on a trip
  7   Bad _____ had prevented John and Rebecca from going to the pool

Read the passage and answer the questions on the following page.

Sam and Matt

Sam Bowers liked to climb trees, and he loved the climbing equipment at the school playground. He hoped to one day become a rock climber. He often day-dreamed that he would be on the news someday because he climbed a huge mountain somewhere. But for now, Sam was in the fifth grade, and he just wanted to safely climb everything he could.

Sam was playing in his backyard one afternoon with his friend Matt. Sam decided to climb the old oak tree in the corner of his yard. Matt climbed another big tree nearby. The two boys climbed into their trees and secured themselves between two branches. They could see each other from their perches.

The boys liked being that high off the ground. Both of the boys liked their spots and decided that next time they would swap trees. Each boy took a piece of string from his pocket and tied it around a nearby branch. That way, the next time they decided to climb the trees, they would know where their spots were.

Sam's mother came to the back door and called for the boys to come inside for lunch. She was very surprised when she saw Matt and Sam climbing out of the trees. She laughed as the boys ran to the door to meet her.

Answer the questions. Circle the letter beside the correct answer.

1. What did Sam like to do?
   A. play with Matt
   B. climb things
   C. play with trees
   D. play in his backyard

2. Where did Matt go when Sam climbed a tree?
   A. to another tree nearby
   B. to his house
   C. to Timmy's house
   D. to his soccer game

3. What did the boys plan to do differently the next time they climb the trees?
   A. wear different shoes
   B. use their two-way radios to talk
   C. swap trees
   D. go to Matt's yard instead

4. Where did the boys go in the trees?
   A. to a secret tree house
   B. to a big limb
   C. to a spot between two branches
   D. just to the second branch

5. What does Sam want to be when he grows up?
   A. a scientist
   B. a rock climber
   C. a musician
   D. an astronaut

6. What reason did the boys have for getting out of the trees?
   A. It was getting dark.
   B. Mr. Bowers needed Sam's help.
   C. They were tired.
   D. Mrs. Bowers called them for lunch.

Read the passage and answer the questions. Circle the letter beside the correct answer.

Hockey

The national sport in Canada is ice hockey. It is a fast and exciting game played on an ice-covered rink. Each team has six players who wear ice skates and try to obtain possession of the puck. Players hold a wooden stick and try to shoot the puck past their opponents into the goal to score points. Unlike other sports, hockey allows each team to substitute players while play is in progress. This helps to maintain the game's fast pace.

A player may commit a foul with his stick or by arguing with an official. When this happens, a player may have to go to the penalty box for a set length of time or for the duration of the game. Hockey games last for sixty minutes. They are played in three segments of twenty minutes each, and the clock runs only while play is going on. Play begins with a face-off between the opposing teams. The winner is the team that scores the most points. Hockey games often end in a tie.

Hockey is fun to watch because of the speed and accuracy of the players. It is popular in the United States, Japan, and Europe, as well as in Canada.

1. Hockey is played on which type of surface?
   A. water   B. ice
   C. clay   D. wood

2. A hockey team is made of _____ players.
   A. 5
   B. 8
   C. 6
   D. 11

3. What rule does hockey have that other sports do not?
   A. A hockey game can end in a tie.
   B. Hockey players can argue with the officials.
   C. Each team can substitute players while play is in progress.
   D. Hockey players usually do not wear uniforms.

4. What is the object of the game of hockey?
   A. to score a field goal   B. to score a goal
   C. to hit the puck the fastest   D. to skate very fast

5. Which country has hockey as its national sport?
   A. United States   B. Italy
   C. Europe   D. Canada

Total Problems: _____   Total Correct: _____   Score: _____

Read the poem and answer the questions. Circle the letter beside the correct answer.

Happiness

My dog licks my face as we roll in the grass,
I hope this playtime will slowly pass.
I slide on the floor with socks on my feet,
Mom has cleaned and it looks very neat.
On hot summer days I go to the beach,
I hope my sand castle is past the waves' reach.
My birthday begins with my breakfast of choice,
I then cheer at the ball game and lose my voice.
Bedtime is welcome to a busy kid like me,
Because I'm usually as active as one child can be.

1. What season makes the author of this poem happy?
    A. winter   B. summer
    C. spring   D. fall

2. Which series of words best describes the poem?
    A. birthday, homework, puppies, sunshine
    B. birthday, breakfast, dog, beach
    C. birthday, ball game, surfing, grades
    D. birthday, bedtime, friends, feet

3. What does the phrase "I hope my sand castle is past the waves' reach" mean?
    A. People are in the waves trying to grab the sand castle.
    B. Water will help the sand castle last a long time.
    C. The person does not want the water to ruin the sand castle.
    D. Ocean animals are trying to get the sand castle.

4. How does the author imply that the person in the poem is tired at the end of a day?
    A. by telling that he or she loses their voice at a ball game
    B. by telling that bedtime is welcome for a busy kid
    C. by telling that the person eats breakfast
    D. by telling that the person slides on the floor

5. The person described in this poem is most likely what age?
    A. 5   B. 25
    C. 2   D. 9

Total Problems: Total Correct: Score:

Name _____

Read the passage and answer the questions on the following page.

Washing Windows

Philip was looking forward to summer. He was tired of homework, book reports, and tests. He would miss seeing his friends every day at school, but that was okay. School was out, and he planned to have a lot of fun. He called his friend Tommy to plan their first outing of the summer. They decided to go bike riding and then do some batting practice at the ball field. The boys were really excited.

Just as Philip was backing his bicycle out of the garage, his mom called to him from the back door. "I need your help, Philip!" she shouted.

Philip reluctantly propped his bike by the front porch and went to see his mom. She began talking about the family's plans to do some cleaning around the house. He listened to what she was saying, and his mind was racing with thoughts of how to end his plans with Tommy. His mom had planned this "cleaning day" several weeks ago, and everyone had promised to help. Philip had forgotten about it and was very disappointed that his plans with Tommy would have to be canceled.

Philip began to mentally prepare his speech for Tommy as he went into the house. He slowly dialed Tommy's number and waited for an answer. Quickly, Philip explained that he would not be able to ride bikes and go to the ball field. Tommy was very understanding, and he asked if it would be okay if he came over to help. Philip was shocked at Tommy's request. Philip checked with his mom, and she said that would be fine. The two of them could wash the windows on the outside of the house.

When Tommy arrived, Philip was out in the front yard with a bucket of soap and water, sponges, and the hose. Tommy parked his bike and joined Philip in front of their first job, the living room window. This was the largest window in the whole house. They began working and quickly saw how their work was paying off. The windows were sparkling in the morning sun. They worked their way to the back of the house and took a break for lunch.

After the windows were cleaned, Philip's father complimented the boys on doing a great job. He offered to take the boys to the ball field for a while and then out for pizza and a movie afterward. The boys were thrilled. Perhaps washing windows wasn't so bad after all!

Name _____

Answer the questions. Circle the letter beside the correct answer.

1. Why was Philip looking forward to summer?
    A.   He wanted to get away from his friends.
    B.   He was planning to get a summer job.
    C.   He was planning to have a lot of fun.
    D.   He hoped to play baseball.

2. Why did Philip have to cancel his plans with Tommy?
    A.   Tommy called and said he couldn't come over.
    B.   He had forgotten about the cleaning jobs.
    C.   It was time for dinner.
    D.   It was time to go inside and get ready for bed.

3. Why did Tommy go over to Philip's house?
    A.   He was very good at washing windows.
    B.   He wanted to help Philip with the cleaning.
    C.   He told Philip it would be more fun to come to his house.
    D.   He wanted to go to a movie.

4. What did the boys wash first?
    A.   the kitchen window
    B.   the living room window
    C.   the bedroom window
    D.   the hall window

5. What did Philip's father offer to the boys?
    A.   an award for being the best window washers in town
    B.   a trip to the movies
    C.   a chance to go to a ball game
    D.   a trip to the ball field, a movie, and a pizza

Total Problems: Total Correct: Score:

Read the paragraph and answer the questions. Circle "True" or "False" beside each statement below.

Ancient Wonders

There are many wonderful things in our world today. Some are natural, while others are man-made. The Greeks and Romans of long ago compiled a list of things they thought were noteworthy. This list contained only man-made objects of great size or unusual quality they considered to be wonders. These objects became known as the Seven Ancient Wonders of the World. They are: the pyramids of Egypt, the Hanging Gardens of Babylon, the Temple of Artemis at Ephesus, the statue of Zeus, the Mausoleum at Halicarnassus, the Colossus of Rhodes, and the Pharos (lighthouse) of Alexandria.

1. The Seven Ancient Wonders of the World are all located in one place. True False

2. The Ancient Wonders are all man-made. True False

3. The Romans and Germans made this list of Ancient Wonders. True False

4. Only large objects or objects of unusual quality were considered wonders. True False

Total Problems: _____ Total Correct: _____ Score: _____

Name _____

Refer to the passage on page 68 to solve the puzzle.

Ancient Wonders Crossword Puzzle

Across

2 The _____ of Artemis
4 There are _____ Ancient Wonders of the World
8 The _____ of Alexandria
10 Where the pyramids are

Down

1 One ancient wonder is a statue of this Greek god
3 The Hanging Gardens of _____
5 Another word for important or special
6 Opposite of man-made
7 Objects of great size or unusual quality were considered to be _____
9 The Romans and _____ compiled the list of wonders

| Total Problems: | Total Correct: | Score: |

Name _____

Read the passage and answer the questions on the following page.

Heidi's Notebook

The bell had just rung. It was eight o'clock. Kids were charging through the hall to their classes. Most of them knew running wasn't allowed, but they still ran. Heidi had put most of her things in her backpack when Neil and John ran past her. Neil's foot accidentally kicked Heidi's notebook and sent it sliding across the floor into Mr. Spencer's classroom.

Heidi stood there in amazement. Everything had happened so fast. After she gathered herself and lifted her backpack to her shoulder, she meekly walked over to Mr. Spencer's class to get her notebook. Suddenly, he closed the door to begin class. Heidi was doomed! Not only was she already late, but now she had to knock on the door to a sixth-grade teacher's class to claim her notebook.

Heidi almost got the courage to knock on the door when, to her surprise, Melinda, a sixth-grade girl she knew, opened the door. She was holding Heidi's notebook. Relieved, Heidi cheerfully greeted Melinda and thanked her for retrieving her notebook. Heidi had been rescued! She didn't have to be embarrassed in front of an entire class of sixth graders. Thank goodness for Melinda! Heidi hurried to her classroom, hoping that her teacher would understand.

Answer the questions. Circle the letter beside the correct answer.

1. Why did Heidi have to go to a sixth-grade classroom?
    A.   She was doing a report.
    B.   She had to retrieve her notebook.
    C.   She was being punished.
    D.   She was looking for Melinda.

2. Where was Heidi's notebook before it was kicked?
    A.   in her hand
    B.   on the floor
    C.   in her locker
    D.   in her bag

3. Who kicked Heidi's notebook?
    A.   Mr. Spencer
    B.   John
    C.   Melinda
    D.   Neil

4. Why was Heidi afraid to get her notebook?
    A.   She was afraid the sixth graders would be mean or laugh.
    B.   She was late to class and didn't want her teacher to know.
    C.   She was hoping to get John to go get the book but was afraid to ask.
    D.   She didn't want to disturb the class.

5. When did Heidi's notebook get kicked?
    A.   before school started
    B.   between classes
    C.   after school
    D.   at lunch

6. How did Melinda make Heidi feel?
    A.   relieved
    B.   frightened
    C.   embarrassed
    D.   unpopular

7. Why did the notebook get kicked?
    A.   It was on the floor, and Heidi forgot about it.
    B.   It was on the floor, and people were running close to it.
    C.   The sixth graders were trying to play a trick on a fourth grader.
    D.   There were no lockers in the school.

Total Problems: ___   Total Correct: ___   Score: ___

Read the passage and answer the questions. Circle the letter beside the correct answer.

Lunar Landing

In 1961, the United States sent *Freedom 7* to make the first trip into space for the country. The astronaut on board was Alan Shepard, a former Navy test pilot who went on to have a long career in space travel. NASA later hired him because of his excellent pilot skills. Mr. Shepard's space flight sent him into orbit on May 5, 1961, only one month after Russia sent a man to orbit the Earth. The United States' voyage began a serious journey into the uncharted region beyond Earth.

Mr. Shepard lay on a padded fiberglass contour couch inside *Freedom 7* for his 116-mile trip beyond the Earth's surface. He returned only fifteen minutes later for a safe landing 300 miles out in the Atlantic Ocean. Ten years later, Mr. Shepard commanded the third trip to the moon for the United States on *Apollo 14*. Due to an illness, Mr. Shepard was unable to travel for the United States space program for six years. This made his return to space on *Apollo 14* that much more special and exciting. Alan Shepard was the fifth American to walk on the moon's surface.

1. Why was Alan Shepard's trip on May 5, 1961, important?
   A. It was his first trip as a pilot.
   B. It was the first space flight for the U.S.
   C. It was a very risky thing to do at that time.
   D. It became a major motion picture.

2. Where did Alan Shepard most likely get his pilot's training?
   A. Army   B. Navy
   C. Air Force   D. NASA

3. Where did Alan Shepard's trip on *Apollo 14* take him?
   A. the moon   B. Mars
   C. Pluto   D. Jupiter

4. What spacecraft did Alan Shepard command in 1971?
   A. *Apollo 14*
   B. *Apollo 13*
   C. *Freedom 7*
   D. *Freedom 8*

5. Why didn't Mr. Shepard travel into space for several years after his 1961 trip?
   A. He was scared of space travel.
   B. He was sick.
   C. He joined the Navy.
   D. He wanted to be a scientist.

Total Problems:	Total Correct:	Score:

Refer to the passage on page 72 to solve the puzzle.

Lunar Landing Crossword Puzzle

Across

3   Alan Shepard commanded this trip to the moon on *Apollo 14*
5   A person who travels into space
9   This country sent a man into space one month before the U.S.
10 Shepard landed in this ocean after his mission in *Freedom 7*

Down

1   Shepard was the _____ American to walk on the moon
2   To travel around
4   The planet on which we live
6   The region beyond the Earth
7   To come back again
8   Shepard was a former Navy _____

| Total Problems: | Total Correct: | Score: |

Read the passage and answer the questions. Circle the letter beside the correct answer.

The Painting on the Ceiling

A magnificent building in Rome is located in the Vatican City. It is called the Sistine Chapel. While it stands only 85 feet tall and measures 134 feet long by 44 feet wide, it is a giant in the history of Catholicism. Erected by Pope Sixtus IV in 1473, it is still used today for the chief ceremonies of the Catholic Church. When a new pope is elected, the Cardinals use the chapel to hold the ceremony.

The walls display marvelous paintings by early Renaissance artists. Many of these depict bits of history. The ceiling is an elaborate scene of stories painted by the artist Michelangelo in the 1500s. He was able to complete the painting after four years of work. Michelangelo also painted the incredible scene in the front of the chapel called *The Last Judgment*. This piece took him eight years to complete. This historic chapel is a destination for many people who visit the ancient and beautiful city of Rome.

1. What is unique about the ceiling in the Sistine Chapel?
    A. It is painted beautiful colors.   B. It has an elaborate scene painted on it.
    C. It is extremely tall.   D. It has very bright lights.

2. How long did it take the artist to complete the painting in the front of the chapel?
    A. seven years   B. four years
    C. six years   D. eight years

3. Who was the artist for the two most famous paintings in the chapel?
    A. Pope Sixtus IV
    B. Michelangelo
    C. Cardinals
    D. Renaissance

4. Where is the Sistine Chapel located?
    A. Vatican City
    B. Paris
    C. St. Ives
    D. Greece

5. What is the Sistine Chapel used for today?
    A. weddings
    B. ceremonies
    C. elections
    D. funerals

Total Problems: ____   Total Correct: ____   Score: ____

Refer to the passage on page 74 to solve the puzzle.

The Painting on the Ceiling Crossword Puzzle

Across

1   Michelangelo was one
5   The Sistine Chapel is still used for these
8   *The Last Judgment* is one
9   The Sistine Chapel is in the _____ City

Down

2   Where the Sistine Chapel is located
3   How many years it took Michelangelo to finish painting the ceiling of the Sistine Chapel
4   Many paintings on the walls of the chapel depict parts of _____
5   Opposite of floor
6   The Pope who erected the Sistine Chapel
7   The Sistine Chapel was erected for the _____ Church

Total Problems:	Total Correct:	Score:

Name _____

Read the passage and answer the questions on the following page.

Honeybees

Honeybees are interesting creatures. They are capable of giving painful stings to humans, but they also provide honey. In fact, they are the only insect that makes a product humans can consume. The organization of the bee community is highly sophisticated. All of the tasks are distributed among the members of the colony, or group, in order to efficiently carry out the work.

Within a colony, scientists have discovered one queen, several drones, and a lot of worker bees. The queen is not responsible for any of the work. The queen is always a very large female and does not even get her own food. That is done for her. She is responsible for the reproduction of the colony. She mates several times a year and produces many offspring. If the queen is not in the hive, the other bees become disorganized and anxious. The queen's fertilized eggs become worker bees, while the unfertilized eggs become drones.

Worker bees are female, and they are always busy gathering food and caring for the young. At a very early age they begin to go out and gather nectar for the hive. No matter how long the trip takes to find food or how far away from the hive the bee is, the route the worker takes back to the hive is the shortest. That is how the term "beeline" came about.

The males are called drones, and they do not work. They are responsible for mating and protecting the queen while the workers gather food. They live only a short time. In autumn, the workers let the drones starve to death because they are no longer useful, and they would eat too much honey during the winter.

Answer the questions. Write a "T" next to each statement that is true. Write an "F" if the statement is false.

1. _____ Worker bees are males and females.

2. _____ The queen keeps the colony organized.

3. _____ Most of the worker bees die in autumn.

4. _____ Drones are male honeybees.

5. _____ Honey made by honeybees is suitable for humans to eat.

Answer the questions below. Circle the letter beside the correct answer.

6. What are the duties of the queen honeybee?
   A. mating, building the hive, protecting the young
   B. mating and keeping the hive organized and busy
   C. gathering food, making honey, and mating
   D. mating and protecting the hive

7. Why do the worker bees travel in a beeline?
   A. The queen expects them to.
   B. It is the shortest distance back to the hive.
   C. They line up behind one another.
   D. They cannot all go into the hive at one time.

8. Which words best describe worker bees?
   A. large, weak, hungry
   B. large, lazy, clumsy
   C. fast, mean, tired
   D. hardworking, busy, caring

9. The queen's eggs become worker bees when:
   A. the eggs are not fertilized
   B. the honey flow is over
   C. the eggs have been fertilized
   D. the weather is cooler

Total Problems: _____ Total Correct: _____ Score: _____

Refer to the passage on page 76 to solve the puzzle.

Honeybees Crossword Puzzle

Across

3   A bee community is called this
6   A type of bee that makes honey
8   A male who protects the queen
9   Drones starve during this season
10   A bug or bee is this type of animal

Down

1   Honeybees make this
2   A bee who reproduces young for the colony
4   Bees gather this to make honey
5   A female who gathers food
7   The gender of all worker bees

Total Problems: Total Correct: Score:

Name _____   Following Directions

In the grid below, find the three items that are alike and in a straight row horizontally, vertically, or diagonally. Draw an oval ring around all three items. Write an "x" on the items that are not like the items in the ring. Write the number of different items that are used in the puzzle. Make a puzzle like this for a friend and explain the directions to him or her.

Number of items: __7__

Answer the questions below. Circle the letter beside the correct answer.

1. The instructions direct you to find three like items in a:
   - (A) row
   - B. box
   - C. ring
   - D. square

2. The second task you are asked to perform is to:
   - A. find three like items
   - B. write an "x" on the other items
   - (C) draw a ring around the three like items
   - D. make a game for a friend

3. Last, the directions instruct you to:
   - (A) make a puzzle like this for a friend
   - B. draw a puzzle with nine items
   - C. draw a ring around the like items
   - D. find the items unlike the others

4. How many different items were used in the puzzle? __7__

5. In what direction did the three like items lie?
   - A. horizontal
   - B. vertical
   - (C) diagonal

© Carson-Dellosa CD-2203

| Total Problems: | Total Correct: | Score: |

9

10

| Total Problems: | Total Correct: | Score: |

Name _____   Following Directions

Read the paragraph and answer the questions. Circle the letter beside the correct answer.

Making Sandwiches

Sara and Jane made peanut butter and jelly sandwiches for a picnic. First, they gathered all of the ingredients they would need and two knives. Next, they took several slices of bread from the bag and placed them on paper plates. Then, they each spread peanut butter on one slice of bread. Next, they each took another slice of bread and spread grape jelly on it. Then, they put the pieces of bread together to make two sandwiches. Finally, they sliced the sandwiches in half and wrapped them in plastic wrap. They made the rest of the sandwiches the same way and finished packing their basket for the picnic.

1. What did the girls do right after spreading the grape jelly on the bread?
   - A. They sliced the sandwiches.
   - B. They placed the sandwiches on a paper plate.
   - (C) The girls put the pieces of bread together, making two sandwiches.
   - D. They packed the picnic basket.

2. What was the very first thing the girls did?
   - A. spread peanut butter on a slice of bread
   - B. took out two slices of bread
   - (C) gathered the ingredients
   - D. took out paper plates and a picnic basket

3. What was the last thing the girls did?
   - A. made peanut butter and jelly sandwiches
   - (B) finished packing their picnic basket
   - C. ate the sandwiches they had made
   - D. selected the pieces of bread

4. Choose the sequence that best describes the girls' actions.
   - A. slice sandwiches, spread peanut butter, pack the basket
   - B. pack the basket, get the ingredients, spread the jelly
   - C. get the bread, spread the jelly, spread the peanut butter
   - (D) spread peanut butter, slice the sandwiches, pack the basket

© Carson-Dellosa CD-2203

Name _____   Finding the Main Idea

Read the paragraphs and answer the questions. Circle the letter beside the correct answer.

Thunderstorm

Sam and Thomas were playing catch in Sam's yard when a loud clap of thunder exploded across the sky. This frightened the boys, so they ran inside. Hard rain soon started to hit the house. Sam's mother was coming downstairs to meet the boys when suddenly all of the lights in the house went out, the television went blank, and the kitchen appliances shut off. "Oh no! The power is out," said Sam. "This is going to ruin our plans for a baseball game!"

1. What is the main idea of the paragraph?
   - A. It is better to be with a friend when the weather is bad.
   - B. Playing outside is always dangerous for children.
   - (C) A thunderstorm was beginning to start in Sam's neighborhood.
   - D. Always play catch away from the windows of a house.

Melissa's Guitar

Melissa's father gave her a guitar for her ninth birthday. She was very excited about learning how to play it. She would often stand in front of her bedroom mirror pretending to be on stage performing for a huge crowd. She began taking guitar lessons from a local music teacher. She surprised her teacher because she learned so quickly. Melissa played some songs she learned at her school talent show. Her friends were also surprised at how well she played. Some of her friends predicted that Melissa would become a rock star one day.

2. What is the main idea of the paragraph?
   - A. Girls can play the guitar as well as boys.
   - (B) Melissa loved to play the guitar.
   - C. Most musicians learn to play the guitar when they are young.
   - D. Everyone can play a musical instrument.

© Carson-Dellosa CD-2203

| Total Problems: | Total Correct: | Score: |

11

12

| Total Problems: | Total Correct: | Score: |

Name _____   Finding the Main Idea

Read the paragraphs and answer the questions. Circle the letter beside the correct answer.

Molly's Birthday

Molly was going to be ten years old on Wednesday. She was very excited about this birthday because she was going to be in the double digits! At school she scribbled all different sizes and kinds of "tens" in her notebook. She wrote some numbers really big and some fat. Then, she colored them in with a marker. Her party was already planned, and she had invited ten friends! It was going to last until ten o'clock Saturday night because she had invited her friends to a movie. The movie would be over at ten o'clock. Molly thought this was going to be the neatest birthday she had ever had.

1. What is the main idea of the paragraph?
   - A. Birthday parties should include a movie.
   - B. Molly is going to get her birthday wish.
   - C. Planning a party can be hard.
   - (D) Molly was excited about her birthday.

Ellie

Ellie was a little black dog who lived with the Sanders family. Mr. and Mrs. Sanders had two children, Mark and Amy. The children loved Ellie very much. Mark liked to play ball with Ellie in the backyard. Amy liked to take Ellie for walks after school. They loved to have her wake them up in the mornings by jumping on their beds and licking their faces. Ellie was a lot of fun to have around! Sometimes Mr. Sanders would pick up treats for Ellie from the pet store on his way home from work. Ellie would greet Mr. Sanders at the door every evening when he came home.

2. What is the main idea of the paragraph?
   - A. Pets are the best companions for children.
   - (B) Ellie was a great dog for the Sanders family.
   - C. Mr. Sanders was a very good pet owner.
   - D. Dogs are better pets than cats.

© Carson-Dellosa CD-2203

Name _____   **Finding Facts**

Read the paragraph and answer the questions. Write an "x" in the blank next to each statement below that is a fact from the paragraph.

The Human Body

The human body is made up of many systems. Each bodily system has a special function to carry out using specific organs and tissues. It is important for good health that all of the systems work together. Each system is made up of one primary organ and other supporting parts. These parts together carry out major body functions. For example, the heart is the primary organ that controls the circulatory system. The blood flows through the veins by way of the heart. All of the organs in these systems are vital for the body to work properly. Organs are so important that doctors work to teach people how to properly care for them and their bodies.

1. __X__ The body needs the organs to carry out special functions.

2. _____ More people have problems with the circulatory system than the digestive system.

3. __X__ The heart is the primary organ in the circulatory system.

4. __X__ Good health exists when all of the systems of the body are working properly.

5. _____ The human body is made up of only one system of organs and tissues.

Total Problems: Total Correct: Score: **13**

Name _____   **Finding Facts**

Read the paragraph and answer the questions. Write an "x" in the blank next to each statement below that is a fact from the paragraph.

William Shakespeare

William Shakespeare is considered the world's greatest literary mind by many notable authorities. Born in England, Shakespeare received little formal schooling. He became fond of the theater when his father's shop was near an old chapel that often opened its doors to traveling actors. William attended some of the shows and enjoyed hearing the lines spoken from the stage. Shakespeare wrote mostly poetry early in his career. He is famous for his sonnets and long narrative poems. Shakespeare became wealthy as a result of his craft. Tax records in England show that at one time he was required to pay nearly five pounds in property tax because he owned so much land. During that time, five pounds was a large sum of money.

1. _____ William Shakespeare was never formally educated.

2. __X__ Shakespeare made money from his works of literature.

3. _____ Shakespeare's father was an actor.

4. __X__ Many of Shakespeare's works include poetry.

5. _____ Shakespeare lived in Scotland.

14   Total Problems: Total Correct: Score:

Name _____   **Figurative Language**

Read the paragraphs and answer the questions. Circle the letter beside the correct answer.

The Science Project

Mandy and Allison decided to do a science fair project together. They selected the topic of photosynthesis. The girls included the three critical science steps: create a hypothesis, follow a procedure, and reach a conclusion. They knew that it would take a long time to complete their science project because each step needed to be carefully carried out. The girls were as busy as bees for the next three weeks as they prepared the project. When they had finished, the girls were very pleased with their work and felt like they had a great chance at winning a ribbon.

1. Why did the author use the phrase "as busy as bees"?
   A. Bees are good subjects for science projects.
   B. People can learn from how bees work.
   C. Bees have certain jobs within colonies and are known as hard workers.
   D. Working reminds the author of bees.

The Bike Ride

David and Lee had been riding their bikes almost all morning on Saturday. They left David's house at nine-thirty A.M. and met their friend Brian for a ride in the park. The three boys raced each other through the trails in the park and up the hill toward Lee's house. Only once during their ride did they stop to rest. Finally, Brian looked at his watch and noticed he had a baseball game in forty-five minutes. After they said good-bye, they all rode off in different directions. David wheeled into his driveway and parked his bike by the back door. He went in the house and found his mother making lunch. "I'm as hungry as a horse," said David. "Thanks for making lunch, Mom!"

2. Why did the author use the phrase "I'm as hungry as a horse"?
   A. Horses are usually hungry after a day of work.
   B. Horses are large animals and they eat a lot.
   C. Boys and horses like the same foods.
   D. David wants a horse of his own someday.

Total Problems: Total Correct: Score: **15**

Name _____   **Figurative Language**

Read the paragraphs and answer the questions. Circle the letter beside the correct answer.

Sandy's Birthday Party

Sandy and her mother were planning Sandy's tenth birthday party. They had chosen a sports theme and had already selected the date for the party. As they continued with their plans, Sandy noticed her soccer schedule had come in the mail. She began looking over the information from her coach and saw that the dates for the tournament had been set. The tournament was going to begin on her birthday! She showed the schedule to her mother and began talking about changing her party plans. It was a good thing she noticed the conflict in the schedule because her mother was about to print the invitations on the computer. "Wow, I would have been in a pickle if I hadn't noticed that tournament date!" said Sandy. She and her mom settled on another date for her party, and they printed her invitations.

1. Why did the author use the phrase "I would have been in a pickle"?
   A. Sandy wanted to have pickles at her birthday party.
   B. Sandy's mother was going to help her make pickles for her birthday party.
   C. It means that someone is in a bad or conflicting situation.
   D. People who get things confused often have more trouble later.

The Hiking Trip

Nicholas was excited about his upcoming hiking trip. He carefully planned for several days before the trip, making sure to take everything he would need. Finally, the day of the trip arrived. He and the other kids in the Outdoor Club loaded the van with all of their gear and headed for the mountains. They spent all of their daytime hours hiking. The group stopped to set up camp each evening at about five-thirty p.m. When the sun came up on the third day, Nicholas was sleeping like a log. He was awakened by some of the other club members as they were packing up their sleeping bags and having breakfast. Today was the trip down the mountain. Nicholas had enjoyed his adventure, but he was growing tired. He was happy to be going home.

2. Why did the author use the phrase "sleeping like a log"?
   A. Logs are motionless, and the phrase implies how still and quiet he was sleeping.
   B. Boys usually pretend to be other things to trick their friends.
   C. Most hikers sleep near logs so it is easy to make a campsite at night.
   D. Everyone was sleeping, including the trees.

16   Total Problems: Total Correct: Score:

Name _____   Drawing Conclusions

Read the paragraphs and answer the questions. Circle the letter beside the correct answer.

A New Adventure

Molly and Jake got up early. They were so excited about the new year ahead. They had chosen their clothes the night before and packed their book bags. After getting dressed, they hurried downstairs to the kitchen to prepare their breakfast. Jake chose cereal, and Molly wanted a bagel. Soon their mother came into the kitchen. She poured a cup of coffee for herself and listened to her children chatter with excitement about their new adventure. Mrs. Murphy reminded her children to brush their teeth. Finally, the bus came down the street. Jake and Molly hurried out to greet it and waved good-bye to their mother.

1. Why do you think Jake and Molly were excited?
    A. It was a holiday.
    B. It was snowing.
    C. They were going on a trip.
    (D) It was the first day of school.

Unpacking

Everyone in the Miller household was busy unpacking boxes and unwrapping treasures that had been in storage for the past eleven months. Susie and John were most excited when Dad began instructing the workers where to place the den furniture. This den was much larger than their old one. Susie and John hurried from room to room to join in on any action they could find. They helped their mother arrange their bedroom furniture and place boxes of clothes beside the closet doors so they could be unpacked. The atmosphere was hectic yet happy for several hours. The family ate pizza later that evening and then went to sleep.

2. What were the family members in the paragraph most likely doing?
    A. decorating their house for a party
    B. preparing for a garage sale
    (C) moving into their new house
    D. getting ready for the first day of school

Total Problems: Total Correct: Score:

17

Name _____   Drawing Conclusions

Read the paragraphs and answer the questions. Circle the letter beside the correct answer.

A Hot Summer Day

Tammy ran into the house after a long, hot afternoon of playing with her friend Sheila. Her mother was beginning to prepare dinner. Tammy liked the smell of hamburger meat cooking in the kitchen. It was Friday, and it had been a great day. Tammy was very thirsty, and her mother asked her if she wanted a drink. "Yes, please," Tammy said. Her mother took a glass from the cabinet and filled it from a bottle she took from the refrigerator. Tammy quickly drank the cool, sweet brown beverage and laughed as the bubbles of carbonation tickled her top lip. This was very refreshing. When she finished her drink, she headed to her room to read before dinner.

1. What was Tammy most likely drinking?
    A. water
    (B) soda
    C. apple juice
    D. orange juice

A Surprise

Laurie and Jay had just gotten home from school when their mother met them in the yard and told them about a surprise. She took them to the backyard, and they noticed a large cardboard box sitting on the patio. The children started to walk toward the box and noticed that the sides were moving slightly. Jay heard a faint whimper coming from the box. The children ran to the box and looked inside. They saw a furry white animal in the corner of the box.

2. What do you think the children saw in the box?
    A. a bird
    (B) a puppy
    C. a cotton ball
    D. a lizard

18

Total Problems: Total Correct: Score:

Name _____   Reading Charts

Use the information in the chart to answer the questions. Write the answers on the lines provided below.

10 Tokens	30 Tokens	50 Tokens
key chain	stuffed animal	sunglasses
note pad	ball	paint set
bubble gum	mouse pad	disguise kit
whistle	joke book	spray string
popcorn	jumbo pencil	action figure
stickers	puzzle	sparkle pen

1. How many tokens are required for a stuffed animal? _____ **30**

2. If Janet has 60 tokens, how many paint sets can she get? _____ **1**

3. Meg has 50 tokens. Can she get a whistle and sunglasses? _____ **no**

4. Sandy has 80 tokens. Can she get a note pad and spray string? _____ **yes**

5. How many tokens are needed to get a key chain and a sparkle pen? _____ **60**

6. How many tokens in all are needed for a puzzle, bubble gum, and popcorn? _____ **50**

7. Jake has 90 tokens. Can he get 2 stuffed animals and an action figure? _____ **no**

8. Robin has 40 tokens. How many 30-token items can she get? _____ **1**

9. Lynn has 20 tokens just for popcorn. How many bags can she get? _____ **2**

10. Dan has 50 tokens. If he gets spray string, will he have any tokens left over? _____ **no**

Total Problems: Total Correct: Score:

19

Name _____   Reading Tables

Use the information in the table to answer the questions. Write the answers on the lines provided below.

Average Monthly Temperatures					
June	July	Aug.	Sept.	Oct.	Nov.
88°	85°	96°	81°	78°	75°

1. Which month(s) was cooler than October? _____ **November**

2. Which month(s) was warmer than September? _____ **June, July, August**

3. What month had an average temperature of 96°? _____ **August**

4. How many months were cooler than June? _____ **4**

5. Which month had an average temperature of 85°? _____ **July**

6. Which month(s) was 3 degrees cooler than June? _____ **July**

20

Total Problems: Total Correct: Score:

Name _____   Reading Graphs

Use the information in the graph to answer the questions. Write the answers on the lines provided below.

Desserts Sold at the Bake Sale

(bar graph: Brownies 30, Cupcakes 25, Cookies 35, Pies 15, Muffins 25)

Desserts

1. How many pies were sold at the bake sale? _____ **15**

2. How many brownies were sold at the bake sale? _____ **30**

3. Which item at the bake sale was the most popular? _____ **cookies**

4. Which item at the bake sale was the least popular? _____ **pies**

5. How many more brownies were sold than muffins? _____ **5**

6. How many fewer pies were sold than cookies? _____ **20**

7. Of the cookies and cupcakes, which sold more? _____ **cookies**

8. Of the muffins and pies, which sold more? _____ **muffins**

9. Twenty-five pieces each were sold of which two desserts? **cupcakes and muffins**

Total Problems:	Total Correct:	Score:

21

© Carson-Dellosa CD-2203

Name _____   A Beautiful Fiber

Read the paragraph. Write a "T" in the blank next to each statement below that is true. Write an "F" if the statement is false.

A Beautiful Fiber

Silk is a shiny, natural fiber. Silk thread is very beautiful and extremely strong. It can stretch and then return to its regular length. It is made from the cocoons of silkworm caterpillars. The production of silk takes place mainly on silk farms. These are places where the worms are kept in clean environments. They are fed fresh leaves and allowed to grow. As they make their cocoons, they use their bodies to create the silk threads that create the cocoon. The silk farmers take a cocoon at this stage and unwrap the one long silk thread. When the threads are made into garments for men and women, the silk is very lightweight and resists wrinkling. Some clothing manufacturers dye silk fabrics in a variety of colors. Dyed silk fabric is usually a much richer color than that of other natural fibers.

1. __T__ Silk is a natural fiber that can stretch.

2. __F__ Silkworms are fed leaves and fruit on silk farms.

3. __T__ The silk thread comes from the silkworm's cocoon.

4. __T__ Silk can be dyed and usually appears richer than other fabrics similarly dyed.

5. __F__ Clothing stores dye their silk fabrics.

22

Total Problems:	Total Correct:	Score:

© Carson-Dellosa CD-2203

Name _____   A Beautiful Fiber

Refer to the paragraph on page 22 to solve the puzzle.

A Beautiful Fiber Crossword Puzzle

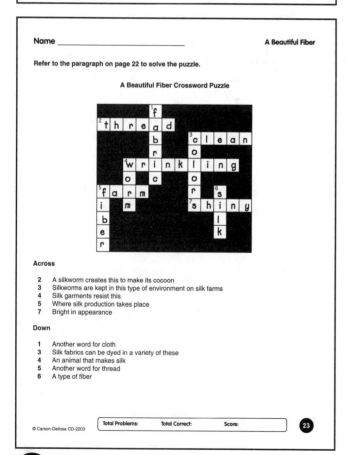

Across

2. A silkworm creates this to make its cocoon
3. Silkworms are kept in this type of environment on silk farms
4. Silk garments resist this
5. Where silk production takes place
7. Bright in appearance

Down

1. Another word for cloth
3. Silk fabrics can be dyed in a variety of these
4. An animal that makes silk
5. Another word for thread
6. A type of fiber

Total Problems:	Total Correct:	Score:

23

© Carson-Dellosa CD-2203

Name _____   Eat Your Veggies!

Read the passage and answer the questions. Circle the letter beside the correct answer.

Eat Your Veggies!

Vegetables are an important source of nutrition. There are many different kinds of vegetables, and it is best to eat a variety with your meals each day. There are different types of vegetables available to us. Some are easily grown in your own backyard. Vegetables like lettuce, cabbage, spinach, parsley, and asparagus are important because of their leaves and the important vitamins and minerals they contribute to a healthy diet. Other vegetables like potatoes, carrots, onions, beets, and turnips grow underground and are the root of the plant. Did you realize you were eating a root the last time you ate a carrot?

When you eat vegetables, you give your body necessary vitamins, like A and C, as well as minerals like calcium and iron. Vegetables do not have a lot of calories, and they don't provide as much energy as other foods do. But, they are helpful in other ways. Beans and peas provide protein when eaten with foods like rice and whole grains. Protein is needed for building muscle and strength.

Vegetables are interesting foods. Some are delicious if eaten raw, while others are better if they are cooked. They come in many different colors, shapes, and sizes. Eating vegetables that are new to you can be a tasty and healthy thing to do!

1. What part of the plant is a carrot?
   A. the stem
   B. the root
   C. the leaf
   D. the flower

2. Why is it important to eat a variety of vegetables?
   A. Some vegetables are better than others.
   B. They are hard to grow.
   C. Vegetables give your body vitamins and minerals.
   D. You would get bored if you ate the same vegetables all the time.

3. Which of the following are leafy green vegetables?
   A. lettuce, cabbage, and spinach
   B. spinach, onions, and parsley
   C. asparagus, lettuce, and potatoes
   D. tomatoes, lettuce, and spinach

24

Total Problems:	Total Correct:	Score:

© Carson-Dellosa CD-2203

Answer Key

Panel 1 (page 25)

Name _____ Eat Your Veggies!

Refer to the passage on page 24 to solve the puzzle.

Eat Your Veggies! Crossword Puzzle

Crossword answers:
- 1 down: vegetable
- 2 across: protein
- 3 down: vitamins
- 4 across: variety
- 5 down: calories
- 6 down: minerals
- 7 across: underground
- 8 down: roots
- 9 across: raw
- 10 across: leaves

Across

2. Needed to build muscle and strength
4. Another word for an assortment
7. Some vegetables grow here
9. Another word for not cooked
10. Spinach, lettuce, and cabbage are important because of these

Down

1. This is an important source of nutrition
3. Vegetables contain _____ and minerals
5. Vegetables do not have a lot of these
6. Some examples of these are iron and calcium
8. Carrots, beets, and turnips are the _____ of the plant

Total Problems: _____ Total Correct: _____ Score: _____   **25**

© Carson-Dellosa CD-2203

Panel 2 (page 26)

Name _____ Tennis, Anyone?

Read the passage and answer the questions on the following page.

Tennis, Anyone?

The game of tennis has been in existence for many years. It is played on a large court with rackets and balls. The players hit the ball back and forth over a net that is in the middle of the court. If two people play tennis against each other, it is called "singles." If four people play at one time, it is called "doubles."

The net in the middle of the court is three feet high. There are different types of outdoor tennis courts. Grass, asphalt, and clay courts are the most common types. Indoor courts are sometimes made of wood or canvas coverings.

The first player to get four points wins the game. Points are counted in a somewhat unusual way. The first point is called 15. The second is 30, and the third is 40. Oddly, the score of zero is called "love" in tennis. The last point is the "game point." It does not have a number. If two players reach 40 at the same time, the first player to get the next two points will win the game. In a large tennis tournament, the players must play a lot of games to win the tournament.

A "set" has been won when a player has won at least six games. Usually, a set has more than six games in it. A match is won when a player wins at least two sets. If the player wins the first two sets, a third set does not have to be played.

Tennis is a very active game that can be played with great skill and athletic ability. Players must practice if they expect to excel at this game. It is possible to become a very good tennis player at a young age. Tennis has a rich history and is full of great men and women players. As with any sport, it is important to have a good attitude toward the other players in the game.

26   © Carson-Dellosa CD-2203

Panel 3 (page 27)

Name _____ Tennis, Anyone?

Answer the questions. Write a "T" in the blank next to each statement below that is true. Write an "F" if the statement is false.

1. **T** Tennis is played on a court.
2. **F** Tennis is not played indoors.
3. **F** The net is located on the side of the court.
4. **T** There are only two players in a singles game of tennis.
5. **T** A player has to get four points to win a game.
6. **T** A set consists of at least six games.
7. **T** Men and women can be good tennis players.

Write your answer to question #8 on the lines provided below.

8. Explain why you think it is important to keep a good attitude toward the other players in any sport.

Answers will vary.

_____
_____
_____
_____
_____
_____
_____
_____

Total Problems: _____ Total Correct: _____ Score: _____   **27**

© Carson-Dellosa CD-2203

Panel 4 (page 28)

Name _____ Hello, Mr. Bell

Read the passage and answer the questions on the following page.

Hello, Mr. Bell

Alexander Graham Bell was a teacher from Scotland who came to the United States to live and work. He taught in Boston, Massachusetts, at a school for deaf children. At home in the evenings he worked on his hobby of making things to help his students. One day in June he was busily working with his partner, Thomas A. Watson, when he accidentally discovered the telephone.

Mr. Bell and Mr. Watson were trying to find a way to make a telegraph that could transmit several messages at one time across a single wire. While Mr. Bell was working in another room, Mr. Watson snapped one of the wooden reeds on the telegraph to loosen it. This caused a change in the electric currents flowing across the wire and actually carried sound. Mr. Bell was so excited. He actually heard Mr. Watson in the other room talking about breaking the reed! Mr. Watson was worried that he had disconnected the telegraph.

Mr. Bell quickly went to find his partner in the other room and tell him what had happened. Both men were fascinated by what they had accomplished. Mr. Bell took his invention to the United States Patent Office to officially register it as his invention. Soon it became known that a long-distance speaking device was available. A doctor in Boston wanted a telephone so that he could speak to his wife at home while he was at his office three miles away. This was the first long-distance telephone installed for a customer.

The telephone quickly became popular. Mr. Bell realized there was a need to continue working on the invention to make it even better. This would make communication between people in different buildings possible. Eventually people would be able to talk to others in different cities.

Today we are able to use the telephone to talk to people in different countries and send faxes and electronic mail messages all because of the original discovery of Alexander Graham Bell on June 2, 1875. We consider the telephone a very important invention, and we rely on it every day.

28   © Carson-Dellosa CD-2203

© Carson-Dellosa CD-2203

83

Name _____   Hello, Mr. Bell

Answer the questions. Circle the letter beside the correct answer. Or, write the answer on the lines provided.

1. What was Mr. Bell's hobby?
   A. making telephones
   B. making telegraphs
   C. making things for deaf students
   D. making patents

2. Where was Alexander Graham Bell from?
   A. Massachusetts
   B. Maine
   C. England
   D. Scotland

3. What was unusual about the invention of the telephone?
   A. It was invented by two men working together.
   B. The inventor was a deaf man.
   C. The invention was supposed to be a larger telegraph.
   D. It was invented in the United States instead of another country.

4. Explain why early customers might have wanted telephones.

   Answers will vary.

5. How is the telephone helpful to us today?

   Answers will vary.

Total Problems: Total Correct: Score: 29

© Carson-Dellosa CD-2203

Name _____   Zachary Taylor

Read the passage and answer the questions on the following page.

Zachary Taylor

Zachary Taylor was the twelfth president of the United States. He was born in Barboursville, Virginia, in 1784. He was the son of Richard and Sarah Taylor. Zachary's father was a plantation owner. As a young boy, Zachary helped his father with the family's farm. He had five brothers and three sisters.

Zachary grew up in the midst of Indian warfare in the 1800s. He did not attend school because there were no schools during that time. He had tutors, and he also learned many lessons by working with his father on the farm. His family was one of the largest slave owners in the South, and later as president of the United States, he opposed freeing the slaves.

Military service was where Zachary Taylor was most effective. He led armies to victory several times in his career. His soldiers nicknamed him "old rough and ready" because he was very skilled at leading troops into battle. He once received a war bonus of six thousand acres of land. He later settled on some of it in Kentucky.

In 1810, Mr. Taylor married a woman named Margaret Smith. They later had a son and five daughters. Zachary Taylor was president for only sixteen months. He became ill in July of 1850 and soon died. His incomplete term was completed by his vice president, Millard Fillmore. During Mr. Taylor's presidency, the United States experienced the Gold Rush of 1849. In addition, the Overland Mail Service and the Office of the Interior were created during this time.

30

© Carson-Dellosa CD-2203

Name _____   Zachary Taylor

Answer the questions. Circle the letter beside the correct answer. Or, write the answer on the lines provided.

1. Zachary Taylor was the _____ U.S. president.
   A. eleventh   B. fourteenth
   C. twelfth   D. second

2. Where did Zachary Taylor get an education?
   A. in school   B. from books
   C. at college   D. at home, from tutors

3. Who were Zachary Taylor's parents?
   A. Margaret and John
   B. Richard and Sarah
   C. Sarah and Thomas
   D. Millard and Elizabeth

4. What is another word for "plantation"?
   A. farm
   B. cabin
   C. town
   D. garden

5. How long did Taylor serve as United States president?
   A. one year, three months
   B. two years
   C. one year, six months
   D. one year, four months

6. Who was Millard Fillmore?
   A. the vice president
   B. the secretary
   C. a soldier in the army
   D. Zachary's father

7. Do you think Zachary Taylor was a good president? Explain why or why not.

   Answers will vary.

Total Problems: Total Correct: Score: 31

© Carson-Dellosa CD-2203

Name _____   Dolly and Brittany

Read the passage and answer the questions on the following page.

Dolly and Brittany

Dolly and Brittany were waiting in the kitchen for their owners, Mr. and Mrs. Moore, to come home when a loud thunderstorm started. The walls of the house seemed to shake with each clap of thunder. This scared the puppies, and they began to whine. The pet gate was wedged in the doorway of the kitchen to keep them from running through the house. Dolly tried several times to push it over. She wasn't strong enough to do that, so she tried biting the wooden frame of the gate.

In the meantime, Brittany was walking back and forth across the kitchen floor. She was very worried and restless. Suddenly, she heard a loud noise and ran to see what it was. Dolly had chewed the pet gate, causing the wooden bar to break and fall out of the doorway. They were free! Both dogs began to bark happily as they scampered down the hall to look for Mr. and Mrs. Moore. They quickly searched all of the bedrooms, but they found no one.

Disappointed, the two dogs went into the den and jumped on the sofa. That's when Dolly noticed a bowl of nuts on the table. She climbed over the edge of the sofa and began eating them out of the bowl. Brittany saw what Dolly was doing and went over to see if any nuts were left. Instead, Brittany found another bowl on the table. It had pretzels! Both dogs ate until the snacks were gone.

Just as they were about to settle down, another clap of thunder shook the house. The rain continued to pummel the house with great force. This upset Dolly and Brittany very much so they began to dig furiously on the sofa. Dolly dug so hard and fast the stuffing began to come out of the cushion. They tried to settle down again, but more noises continued to disturb them. The telephone rang, the clock in the hall chimed, and cars drove down the street.

Just then, the front door opened. It was Mr. and Mrs. Moore! Mr. Moore let his wife inside while he shook his umbrella on the porch. Brittany, trying to get to the door, jumped off the sofa. Her feet bumped the table so hard that the lamp and bowls came crashing to the floor. Mrs. Moore heard the loud noise and saw Brittany running to greet her.

Mr. Moore looked at the dogs and said, "Just what have you been up to lately?" The dogs just sat there, trying to look as cute as possible. Mr. and Mrs. Moore hung up their wet coats and umbrella and started toward the den. They had no idea what they were about to find!

32

© Carson-Dellosa CD-2203

84

© Carson-Dellosa CD-2203

Name _____   Dolly and Brittany

Answer the questions. Write the answers on the lines provided.

1. What is this story about?
   The story is about two dogs who are at home alone during a thunderstorm. They become scared and make a mess in the den. The story ends as the owners come home and walk towards the den.

2. Who are the characters in this story?
   Two dogs, Dolly and Brittany, and their owners, Mr. and Mrs. Moore, are the characters.

3. What is the setting for this story?
   The home of Mr. and Mrs. Moore. The dogs escape from the kitchen and damage the den, where most of the action takes place.

4. What is the problem in this story?
   The dogs create a mess by damaging a dog gate and a sofa. They eat food left in the den and knock over a lamp and bowls.

5. Why are the people in the story going to be surprised?
   Mr. and Mrs. Moore will be surprised to see the damage the dogs have done in the den.

© Carson-Dellosa CD-2203   Total Problems: Total Correct: Score: **33**

Name _____   Aunt Mary's Baby

Read the passage and answer the questions on the following page.

Aunt Mary's Baby

My Aunt Mary is going to have a baby soon. I am so excited because I live down the street from her, and I can visit the baby whenever I want. My mom is Aunt Mary's sister. Mom says it is going to be great having a new little cousin. I have two older brothers, Lee and Ryan. They are huge baseball fans. I am the only girl, and I like sports, too. My name is Joanna, and I like being the youngest in my family.

Aunt Mary and Uncle Kyle plan to name their baby Ethan if it is a boy and Nicole if it is a girl. I like those names. I hope it is a girl. I went to Aunt Mary's house almost every day for about three weeks this summer. I was helping her get the baby's room ready. I helped put the clothes in the drawers, hang pictures on the walls, and put sheets and blankets in the crib. I also put all of the stuffed animals on a bookshelf in the baby's room for the baby to see when he or she is awake. Aunt Mary said a baby's room is sometimes called a nursery. This nursery is certainly the cutest I have ever seen.

When the baby gets home, he or she will sleep a lot. Aunt Mary and Uncle Kyle will have to feed the baby often and change diapers, too. Their dog Coco may become jealous of the baby because of all the attention he or she will receive. Coco has never seen a baby before. I think Coco will like the baby. When the baby can play and walk, Coco will have lots of fun!

I sometimes feel like time is going by so slowly, and the baby will never arrive. But, Mom tells me that it will be here before we know it. I will go to Aunt Mary's house every day so the baby will know who I am. It will be so much fun!

34   © Carson-Dellosa CD-2203

Name _____   Aunt Mary's Baby

Answer the questions. Circle the letter beside the correct answer. Or, write the answer on the lines provided.

1. Who is having a baby?
   A. Nicole   B. Mom
   (C.) Mary   D. Coco

2. This story is being told by:
   (A.) a young girl   B. a mother
   C. a boy   D. a baby

3. Why did Joanna visit Aunt Mary during the summer?
   A. She watched the baby for her aunt.
   (B.) She helped decorate the baby's room.
   C. She took care of the dog.
   D. She looked for her brothers.

4. If the baby is a boy, what will they name it?
   A. Lee   B. John
   (C.) Ethan   D. Ryan

5. Why might the dog become jealous of the baby?
   A. It has never seen a baby.
   B. Babies do not like dogs.
   (C.) The baby will receive a lot of attention.
   D. There was not a dog in this story.

6. What did the story mention that new babies often do?
   A. cry
   B. eat
   (C.) sleep
   D. play

7. Describe how you think the author feels about having a new baby cousin.
                    Answers will vary.

© Carson-Dellosa CD-2203   Total Problems: Total Correct: Score: **35**

Name _____   July

Read the poem and answer the questions. Circle the letter beside the correct answer.

July

I'll jump into the swimming pool,
I hope to find it comfortably cool.
The sun is hot and the air is dry,
Fluffy, white clouds float on by.
Summer is so much fun for me,
This is exactly how I like to be.
Schedules and homework are gone away,
I laugh and play with friends each day.
Vacations end but memories last,
The summer passes way too fast.

1. What is the main idea of this poem?
   A. The author likes to swim.
   B. You see many kinds of clouds in the summer.
   (C.) The author enjoys summer for many reasons.
   D. Funny things happen at a pool.

2. Why does the poem say that homework has gone away?
   (A.) It is summer, and there is no school or homework.
   B. He is dreaming that there will not be any homework.
   C. He lost his homework and hopes the teacher will not know.
   D. Homework is too hard.

3. What does the poem say will last after summer is over?
   A. clouds   (B.) memories
   C. vacations   D. friends

4. How many lines does the poem have?
   A. 8   B. 7
   (C.) 10   D. 12

5. In this poem every _____ lines rhyme.
   A. 4   (B.) 2
   C. 6   D. 8

6. The author of this poem is most likely what age?
   A. 22   (B.) 10   C. 2   D. 30

36   Total Problems: Total Correct: Score: © Carson-Dellosa CD-2203

© Carson-Dellosa CD-2203

85

Name _____ July

Refer to the poem on page 36 to solve the puzzle.

July Crossword Puzzle

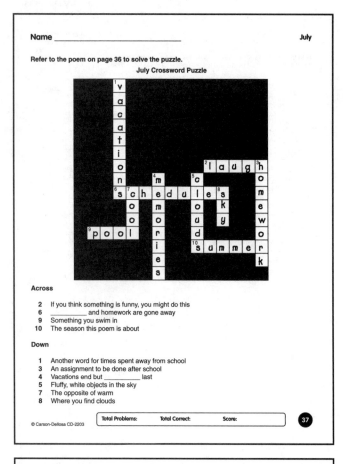

Across

2 If you think something is funny, you might do this
6 _____ and homework are gone away
9 Something you swim in
10 The season this poem is about

Down

1 Another word for times spent away from school
3 An assignment to be done after school
4 Vacations end but _____ last
5 Fluffy, white objects in the sky
7 The opposite of warm
8 Where you find clouds

© Carson-Dellosa CD-2203   Total Problems: Total Correct: Score: **37**

Name _____ Jacques Cousteau

Read the passage and answer the questions on the following page.

Jacques Cousteau

A pioneer is a person who does something new before anyone else. He or she may travel to a new place or discover something no one else has discovered. We often read about the brave pioneers of our country and the explorers who discovered how huge the new land of America was. However, there is another world we often forget. It is the ocean. Under the waves lies a vast region of sea life and unusually shaped places. There are pioneers of underwater places, too!

A famous man named Jacques Cousteau was a pioneer of the underwater world. He was French, and he made some wonderful and helpful discoveries under the sea. He swam very well and took pictures of underwater life. Many people had never seen this before, so it was very exciting. Jacques Cousteau was also a great writer. He often wrote about his diving experiences. He even made a movie about what he had learned. The movie, *The Silent World*, won an Academy Award.

Exploring the ocean was a big thrill for Jacques Cousteau. But, he knew it would be easier to explore if he could hold his breath longer, or invent a way to take extra oxygen with him. This desire caused him to invent the Aqua-Lung™, or S.C.U.B.A. (self-contained underwater breathing apparatus). This is a large tank filled with oxygen that divers wear when they explore the underwater world. The Aqua-Lung™ made diving much easier. Divers could stay under the water longer and get more information on their trips.

Jacques Cousteau continued to dive until he reached the age of seventy-five. He was very intelligent and had so much experience that younger dive crews would ask him to ride with them during an exploration. His experience and knowledge was a valuable aid to divers and scientists as they learned about the underwater world.

38   © Carson-Dellosa CD-2203

Name _____ Jacques Cousteau

Answer the questions. Circle the letter beside the correct answer.

1. What did Jacques Cousteau do?
   A. He explored America.
   B. He explored the ocean.
   C. He invented boats.
   D. He liked to fish.

2. Where was Jacques Cousteau from?
   A. England
   B. America
   C. France
   D. Italy

3. What diving tool did he invent?
   A. the bathing suit
   B. the S.C.U.B.A. tank
   C. the camera
   D. the Academy Award

4. According to the passage, what other talent did Jacques Cousteau have?
   A. singing
   B. writing
   C. cooking
   D. flying

5. According to the passage, what is a pioneer?
   A. Someone who explores oceans.
   B. A person who travels to a new place first or discovers something new.
   C. People who want to move to a new house.
   D. Divers who want to take pictures under water.

6. Why did younger divers want Mr. Cousteau to go on trips with them?
   A. They needed him to drive the boat.
   B. They needed to use his S.C.U.B.A. equipment.
   C. They knew he could make the trip into a movie.
   D. He knew a lot about the sea and diving.

7. What was the name of the movie Jacques Cousteau made?
   A. *The Water World*   B. *The Best Ocean*
   C. *The Silent World*   D. *The Fish and Me*

© Carson-Dellosa CD-2203   Total Problems: Total Correct: Score: **39**

Name _____ Hawaii

Read the paragraph and answer the questions. Circle the letter beside the correct answer.

Hawaii

Hawaii is the only U.S. state that does not lie on the mainland of North America. It is made up entirely of islands in the Pacific Ocean. It is also the southernmost state in the United States. The primary religion of Hawaii is Roman Catholic. Some Asian families of Hawaii are worshipers of the Buddhist religion. Farming is a big business on the islands. The soil is very fertile for planting various crops. The climate is warm year-round which makes a longer growing season possible. Hawaii also has a large tourist industry. It is a popular destination for people who like the beach and history. Hawaii was first inhabited by the Polynesians. In later years, other races and nationalities have moved to the islands. The beautiful flowers and Hawaiian dancers are notable features of the state. Most people fly to the Hawaiian islands from the United States and other places. Boats are also often used.

1. Hawaii is made of _____.
   A. mainland   **B. islands**
   C. mountains   D. oceans

2. Hawaii is located in the _____ Ocean.
   A. Indian
   B. Polynesian
   C. Pacific
   D. Atlantic

3. What are two large industries in Hawaii?
   A. tourism and farming
   B. farming and fishing
   C. boating and fishing
   D. trading and travel

4. A reasonable explanation for the beautiful flowers in Hawaii is:
   A. Many scientists live there and study the way to grow flowers all year.
   B. The fertile soil and the warm, year-round temperatures provide ideal conditions.
   C. The tourist industry provides enough money for the state to buy nice flowers.
   D. Many residents of Hawaii have their own gardens.

5. According to the paragraph, why would people be interested in visiting Hawaii?
   A. beautiful beaches, history, and warm climate
   B. beautiful churches, farming, and nice hotels
   C. excellent schools, good economy, and good location
   D. good restaurants, excellent jobs, and good pay

40   Total Problems: Total Correct: Score: © Carson-Dellosa CD-2203

Worksheet 1 (Page 41)

Name _____ Portugal

Read the passage and answer the questions. Write a "T" in the blank next to each statement below that is true. Write an "F" if the statement is false.

Portugal

I am visiting a new place this summer with my grandparents. It is Lisbon, Portugal. Portugal is small compared to the United States. In fact, it is only a little larger than the whole state of Maine. The people here speak Portuguese, which is a lot like Spanish. Spain is very close to Portugal, so there are some things in Portugal that are like Spain.

Some people who live here fish, and others help with trading goods to other countries. Fishing and bringing in fresh seafood are big jobs in Portugal. Some families have farms and grow things to sell. There are also famous wine makers in the country, and fruits are grown here, too. We have eaten delicious fruit desserts every night after dinner. We've eaten a lot of seafood here, too.

I have enjoyed my visit to Portugal. I can't wait to get back to the United States and tell my friends about the things we have seen. I hope we can get our pictures developed quickly. When I return to school, I might do a report on Portugal for my teacher. I will have a lot to tell and pictures to go with it! This has been a really fun vacation.

1. __T__ The fishing industry is very important in Portugal.

2. __T__ Spanish is somewhat like Portuguese.

3. __F__ Many people in Portugal work for large banks.

4. __T__ The person telling this story is most likely a child.

5. __F__ The characters in this story are from Spain.

6. __F__ Portugal is smaller than Maine.

7. __T__ Fruits are grown in Portugal.

Total Problems: _____ Total Correct: _____ Score: _____

41

© Carson-Dellosa CD-2203

Worksheet 2 (Page 42)

Name _____ Basketball Camp

Read the passage and answer the questions on the following page.

Basketball Camp

My friend Jake and I love to play basketball. This fall we are going to go to a basketball camp on Saturdays. It is going to last all day. We are very excited. I have a basketball hoop in my driveway at home. Jake comes over every day after school, and we play together. I am better at layups than him. He is taller than I am, so his jump shot is better than mine. We have other interests in common, too, but basketball is our favorite. My name is Blake. My dad calls us the "basketball akes" because both of our names end with the letters "a", "k", and "e." He thinks he is so funny!

When we get to camp, the leaders will divide us into groups. I guess that is like being on teams. We will go to different courts both in the gymnasium and outside to practice drills and game strategies. I hope that Jake and I will be in the same group. I want to learn how to be a better basketball player.

After several Saturdays, we are going to play a game with other groups. The winners of those groups will then play each other. This is like a tournament. The last winning team is the champion! I know that it would be a lot of fun to win, but learning about the game will be fun for me. All of the kids were told that at the end of the camp a famous basketball player is going to come and meet us. No one knows who it is. Jake and I hope it is Michael Jordan. We think he is the best basketball player of all time! This is going to be a great camp. I can't wait until Saturday gets here. I am ready to go! I know Jake is, too.

42

© Carson-Dellosa CD-2203

Worksheet 3 (Page 43)

Name _____ Basketball Camp

Answer the questions below. Circle the letter beside the correct answer. Or, write the answer on the lines provided.

1. When are the boys going to basketball camp?
   A. next summer   **B.** on Saturdays
   C. after school   D. next year

2. What does Blake hope to learn at camp?
   A. how to get along with others   B. how to play on a good team
   C. how to play better basketball   D. how to coach basketball

3. Where will the groups practice their game strategies?
   A. outside   B. inside
   C. outside and inside   D. at home

4. What skill is Jake better at than Blake?
   A. jump shots   B. free throws
   C. layups   D. passing

5. What special game is going to be played at the end of the camp?
   A. championship   **B.** tournament
   C. scramble   D. match

6. Who is going to visit the kids at the camp?
   A. a famous basketball player   B. their parents
   C. no one   D. their teachers

7. On the lines below write a paragraph about a sport you like or have seen being played. Use descriptive words to make your paragraph interesting.

Answers will vary.

Total Problems: _____ Total Correct: _____ Score: _____

43

© Carson-Dellosa CD-2203

Worksheet 4 (Page 44)

Name _____ House Hunting

Read the passage and answer the questions on the following page.

House Hunting

Melanie Miller and her parents flew into Chicago last night. The Millers are moving because Melanie's father received a job promotion. This is exciting and a little scary because Melanie doesn't know anyone in the new place. After breakfast today, the Miller family will begin their search for a new house.

Mr. Miller has to work in the city, but Mrs. Miller hopes to find a house in the suburbs. Melanie wants to find a neighborhood that has a lot of kids. She is even hoping there is a community swimming pool nearby. The Miller's old neighborhood in Atlanta, Georgia, had the best pool, and Melanie knew every kid on her street. Mrs. Miller tried to reassure her daughter that the process of making friends would take awhile. They had lived at their old house for nine years, so it was no surprise that Melanie felt so comfortable there and knew so many people.

The family finished their breakfast in the hotel restaurant and went to the lobby to meet their real estate agent. Mrs. Jenkins told the Millers she was very excited to see them. She was anxious to get started because there were several houses she wanted to show them.

The first one was a large, red brick house with huge bedrooms and lots of closets. The kitchen was big and fancy. Mrs. Miller was not sure she needed a kitchen that big. The next house they looked at was also large and had several rooms, a basement, and a big backyard. The third house had two fireplaces and a living room that was large enough to hold three sofas! Melanie had never seen a house that big before. The ceilings were really high, and the rooms seemed to have an echo. The last house they saw also had a basement, and the bedrooms all had private bathrooms. Melanie liked the idea of having a basement. It would be one more room for her books and games. It was very big, and her father said the house even had enough room for him to have a small office.

Melanie liked all of the houses Mrs. Jenkins showed her family. Now it was up to her parents to talk it over and decide where the family should live. Finally, they decided on the second house they had seen. It was the one with a basement and a huge backyard. Mr. and Mrs. Miller finished talking to Mrs. Jenkins, and they signed the contract before they left. When they got back to the hotel, Mrs. Miller suggested that they go play miniature golf. Melanie and her father liked that idea, so they went.

44

© Carson-Dellosa CD-2203

87

Name _____   House Hunting

Answer the questions. Circle the letter beside the correct answer.

1. Why is the Miller family moving to a new house?
   (A) Mr. Miller has a new job in a different town.
   B. Mrs. Miller wanted to move to the suburbs.
   C. Their old house was too small for them.
   D. They didn't have a swimming pool.

2. How long did the Millers live in Atlanta, Georgia?
   A. five years
   B. two years
   C. eight years
   (D) nine years

3. Where did the Miller family see Mrs. Jenkins?
   A. Atlanta
   (B) Chicago
   C. Boston
   D. New York

4. How many houses did the Millers see on their house-hunting tour?
   (A) four
   B. three
   C. five
   D. one

5. Why did Melanie like the idea of having a house with a basement?
   (A) She could have a special place to play.
   B. It made the house seem larger.
   C. Her father needed an office.
   D. Houses with basements always have larger yards.

6. Which house did the family decide to buy?
   A. the first one
   (B) the second one
   C. the fifth one
   D. the fourth one

Total Problems: Total Correct: Score: **45**

© Carson-Dellosa CD-2203

Name _____   Another Use for Seeds

Read the passage and answer the questions on the following page.

Another Use for Seeds

Karsen got off the school bus still puzzled by her teacher's art assignment. Just hours ago she was sitting in Mrs. Pennington's art class listening to her teacher explain the next assignment. The teacher explained that she wanted each student to "artfully present" his or her own house. Karsen immediately thought of her collection of markers, crayons, colored pencils, and watercolors. She could make a very artful presentation with the huge range of colors she had to choose from. She was sure this project would be a breeze. However, Mrs. Pennington then said that no crayons, paints, or markers could be used. Karsen and her classmates were stunned! This would be impossible. How could they draw without those materials?

Several students asked questions, but Mrs. Pennington simply answered that everyone should use their imagination. Class ended and it was time to go to lunch. Karsen, Leah, and Sonya sat together at lunch chatting about the strange art assignment. Leah said she was going to ask her father for help since he was an architect. Leah said her grandmother was always doing crafts, so she was planning to ask her.

When Karsen arrived home, her little brother Dylan had to go to his soccer game. Karsen didn't want to go but her mother encouraged her to come with them because her father was going to meet them at the game. While Dylan played, Karsen headed to the concession stand to get a snack. Karsen got a drink and a package of sunflower seeds and went back to join her mother. Soon her dad arrived, and they watched the game and chatted about school. Karsen told her parents about the weird art assignment and asked for suggestions. Her father agreed to help her after the game.

Still bothered about not having an idea, Karsen began playing with her empty sunflower seed shells. She began placing them in rows and circles on the seat beside her. She quickly noticed that the seeds could create a picture. And, seeds come in different colors. She could make a mosaic using seeds! Karsen was excited about her discovery and began planning her project. She would use pumpkin seeds for the white painted wood on their house and corn seeds for the yellow shutters. Her mind was racing with great ideas.

This was an original idea. Now the project would be fun to do. At home that evening Karsen's father came up to her room to help her with the project as he had promised. Karsen told him her idea and said that he could help her glue the seeds to the paper. Karsen got all of the paper and materials she would need for the project, and they began working.

46

© Carson-Dellosa CD-2203

Name _____   Another Use for Seeds

Answer the questions. Circle the letter beside the correct answer.

1. What did Karsen have to create for art class?
   A. a painting of her pet
   (B) a picture of her house
   C. a drawing of her family
   D. a model of her school

2. Why did Mrs. Pennington not want the students to use the usual art supplies?
   A. She wanted them to use recycled material.
   B. She didn't have many of the art supplies.
   (C) She wanted the students to use their imaginations.
   D. She was trying to follow the rules for the art contest.

3. How did Karsen come up with the idea of using seeds in the picture?
   A. Her father told her to use them.
   B. Her friends were using seeds, so she decided to do that also.
   (C) She got the idea from playing with her empty sunflower seeds.
   D. She saw the idea on television.

4. Why did Karsen go to the soccer game?
   A. She was very interested in the sport.
   (B) Her dad was going to be there.
   C. Her brother had a game.
   D. She wanted sunflower seeds.

5. According to the context clues, the word "mosaic" most likely means:
   A. likeness
   B. made of seeds
   C. colorful
   (D) picture or design

Total Problems: Total Correct: Score: **47**

© Carson-Dellosa CD-2203

Name _____   Holiday Shopping

Read the passage and answer the questions. Circle the letter beside the correct answer.

Holiday Shopping

Katie and Lisa love to go holiday shopping with their mothers. They had been saving their baby-sitting money so that they wouldn't have to ask their parents for spending money this year. The girls were more excited than ever! They were planning to go the day after Thanksgiving and be there in the morning when the mall opened. That way they would get to the stores while the merchandise was still folded and ready for shoppers. Katie's favorite stores are specialty clothing stores with cool clothes. Lisa prefers the department stores where there are clothes, jewelry, and makeup. The girls wanted to go to as many stores as possible this year. This was going to be a great shopping trip.

Katie called Lisa that morning, and the girls chatted eagerly about their plan for the day. The girls decided to meet at Lisa's house and ride with their mothers to the mall. Lunch would be at the food court. After shopping, they would return to Lisa's house and order a pizza.

Lisa's mom drove everyone to the mall and parked near the department store entrance. Everyone decided to meet at the water fountain in the center of the mall at twelve-thirty to eat lunch and again at four-thirty to return home. Katie and Lisa would be on their own for shopping. Lisa wanted to find a gift for her grandmother and her little brother Joey. Katie wanted to look for gifts for her father and her sister Michelle.

1. Who are the main characters in this story?
   A. Kate and Lisa   (B) Katie and Lisa
   C. Kelly and her mom   D. Lisa and Katie's parents

2. When did the girls go on their shopping trip?
   (A) after Thanksgiving   B. after the holidays
   C. summer   D. spring

3. Where did the girls go shopping?
   (A) the mall
   B. the shopping center
   C. the music store
   D. the computer place

4. Why was this shopping trip different than ones in the past?
   A. The girls were going to be allowed to eat lunch by the fountain.
   B. The girls were allowed to stay all day at the mall.
   (C) The girls had their own money to spend.
   D. The girls went without their mothers.

48   Total Problems: Total Correct: Score:

© Carson-Dellosa CD-2203

Mr. FBI

Name _____ Mr. FBI

Read the passage and answer the questions. Write the answers on the lines provided.

Mr. FBI

When you think of the FBI, visions of uniformed sharp shooters probably come to mind. While they are a vital part of the Federal Bureau of Investigation, they are just one part. The bureau, commonly known by its initials, is a government organization that focuses on eliminating organized crime and dealing with public enemies. The bureau was staffed with untrained men in its beginning. That changed in 1924, when a man named J. Edgar Hoover took over the top-ranked position. He replaced the less-skilled employees with lawyers and accountants.

As a lawyer himself, Mr. Hoover knew how valuable legal knowledge was in fighting crime. He had a vision for the United States. He wanted a strong agency to tackle crime and help local police precincts in their battles against crime. He got just that. Mr. Hoover led the FBI from 1924 to 1972. During that time, he developed ways to identify criminals and solve even the toughest cases. He helped develop ways to use human fingerprints to identify criminals. He began the huge task of getting police stations to become more organized. He also developed ways to use technology and laboratories to solve unusual crimes.

1. According to the story, who is credited with building up the FBI?

   J. Edgar Hoover

2. What were some of the changes he brought to the agency?

   hired skilled employees, developed ways to identify criminals and solve tough cases, helped develop fingerprint identification, encouraged organization in police stations, developed ways to use technology to solve unusual crimes

3. What did he want the local polices stations to do?

   become more organized

4. How long was Hoover in charge of the government agency?

   48 years

5. What profession did Mr. Hoover have originally?

   lawyer

© Carson-Dellosa CD-2203

Total Problems:	Total Correct:	Score:

49

Accidental Inventions

Name _____ Accidental Inventions

Read the passage and answer the questions. Circle the letter beside the correct answer. Or, write the answer on the lines provided.

Accidental Inventions

Inventions sometimes happen by mistake. For instance, an inventor might have an idea for a new device. As it is being developed, the inventor might realize that there could be another use for the tool. It may be a completely different use than he or she first imagined. Creating a new tool, machine, or toy can be a long or short process. Of course, more complex inventions normally will take a longer time to create.

Once an invention is designed and there is a valid purpose for it, the inventor show it to other people to determine if it could be manufactured and sold to the public. That is how many inventions become common household products. Imagine what your life would be like without a vacuum cleaner, a telephone, or a lamp! We use so many inventions each day that we often forget or overlook their value to us.

Once the item has been created, the inventor may want to protect the idea and the invention by getting a patent. This is a legal way of saying that the idea and invention belong to the inventor.

1. Why are some inventions created by accident?

   During the development process, the inventor might realize there could be another use for the invention.

2. A person who invents things is called a(n) _____.
   A. genius   (B.) inventor
   C. invention   D. scientist

3. Name several inventions you use in your home.

   Answers will vary.

4. How long should it take to invent something?
   A. about two months   B. about one year
   (C.) no specific time limit   D. only a few weeks

5. Why is it a good idea to get a patent for an invention?
   A. You can show it to your friends.   B. It is not expensive.
   (C.) It will protect your idea.   D. It will be easier to sell your idea.

50

Total Problems:	Total Correct:	Score:

© Carson-Dellosa CD-2203

Rain

Name _____ Rain

Read the poem and answer the questions. Circle the letter beside the correct answer. Or, write the answer on the lines provided.

Rain

The water feels fresh and clean on my face;
It makes me slow to a careful pace.
The puddles surprise my feet as I walk;
I like how the noises cover the talk.
I hold my umbrella and walk to the door,
Then place my galoshes on the floor.
It feels all cozy and warm inside;
I sit by the fire and pretend to hide.
From the misty outdoors to the warm pleasures here,
The reasons I'm home are perfectly clear.

1. What does the author mean by the phrase "makes me slow to a careful pace"?
   (A.) It is difficult to walk in the rain, so the author is careful.
   B. The author likes walking in the rain and getting wet.
   C. The author is really taking a shower.
   D. Rain always makes people walk much slower than normal.

2. What does the author mean by the phrase "the puddles surprise my feet as I walk"?
   A. The author's feet don't know that it is raining.
   (B.) The author's feet suddenly get wet, which is like a surprise.
   C. The author's feet are tricked by the puddles of water on the ground.
   D. The author accidentally fell into a puddle of water.

3. How do you think the author feels at home?
   A. unhappy
   (B.) pleased
   C. lonely
   D. tired

4. On the lines below describe an experience you've had in the rain.

   Answers will vary.

© Carson-Dellosa CD-2203

Total Problems:	Total Correct:	Score:

51

Leave It to the Leaves

Name _____ Leave It to the Leaves

Read the passage and answer the questions. Circle the letter beside the correct answer.

Leave It to the Leaves

Leaves are the food-producing part of plants. They act as little "factories" for making food for the plant. Most leaves are flat and green. The leaf contains a green chemical called chlorophyll, which is necessary in the process of making food. This food-making process is called photosynthesis. In this process, the chlorophyll in the leaf reacts when sunlight contacts it. The wide, flat leaf makes it easy for sunlight to shine on the leaf blade. Carbon dioxide combines with the water in this process, and ultimately, food is made for the plant.

Once the food is made in the leaves, the plant may store the food in the stem, roots, fruit, or seeds. Leaves vary in shape and size. Some plants have many leaves, while others have only a few. Grass is an example of a very common, long narrow leaf. A blade of grass is a leaf. Inside each leaf is a system of tiny veins which transport the plant's nutrients. Grass blades have parallel veins. Some leaves have veins that branch out and form a wide or oval leaf blade. Leaves are vital to the life of every plant.

1. How are leaves like factories?
   A. They make new plants.   B. They make flowers.
   (C.) They make the plant's food.   D. They make fruits.

2. What is the green chemical in leaves that is necessary for making food?
   A. chloroplasts   (B.) chlorophyll
   C. veins   D. fruit

3. Where might a plant store food?
   A. stem, roots, soil, leaves   (B.) stem, roots, fruit, seeds
   C. bud, stem, branches, flower   D. stem, leaf, bark, petal

4. Long, narrow leaves have what type of vein arrangement?
   (A.) parallel
   B. wide
   C. narrow
   D. round

5. What does a leaf need to make food for a plant?
   A. carbon dioxide, sunlight, water, and grass
   (B.) carbon dioxide, water, sunlight, chlorophyll
   C. carbon dioxide, roots, leaves, sunlight
   D. carbon dioxide, stems, veins, sunlight

52

Total Problems:	Total Correct:	Score:

© Carson-Dellosa CD-2203

Name _____   Leave It to the Leaves

Refer to the passage on page 52 to solve the puzzle.

Leave It to the Leaves Crossword Puzzle

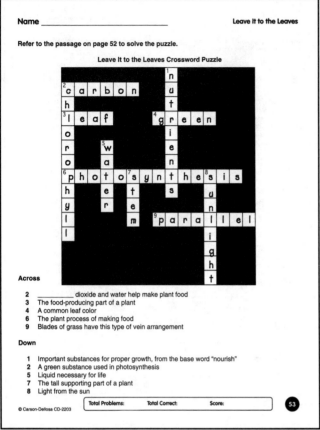

Across

2 _____ dioxide and water help make plant food
3 The food-producing part of a plant
4 A common leaf color
6 The plant process of making food
9 Blades of grass have this type of vein arrangement

Down

1 Important substances for proper growth, from the base word "nourish"
2 A green substance used in photosynthesis
5 Liquid necessary for life
7 The tall supporting part of a plant
8 Light from the sun

© Carson-Dellosa CD-2203 | Total Problems: | Total Correct: | Score: | 53

Name _____   Nancy's Office

Read the passage and answer the questions on the following page.

Nancy's Office

Nancy is ten years old. Her bedroom is upstairs in her family's house. Nancy loves her room, but it is full of stuff. Her mom is always telling her to straighten it up and make it look neater. She can usually tidy up enough to make her mom happy, but her room is never really organized. Nancy wanted to be organized. She just didn't know how. She knew it would be easier to find things if everything had a place. This would be a good project for her.

Nancy went to her father's office one day after school and waited in the lobby for him to take her home. Her father was in a meeting, so she had several minutes to wait. She began talking with Cheryl, a woman who worked with her dad. Cheryl had a very neat desk with drawers on the side and file cabinets behind her. When she received phone calls each day, she kept the messages in a neat stack. Whenever she needed a paper, she could find it in a file. Cheryl's office was very organized!

Nancy noticed everything Cheryl did. She asked Cheryl a lot of questions about her office and how she set up everything. Cheryl explained how she filed papers, kept supplies in drawers, and threw away things she no longer needed. Cheryl explained that when her desk was messy, it was often because she had not thrown away things that were old.

Nancy thought about this and made mental plans about how she could make her own "office" at home and organize all of her stuff. Nancy rode home with her father that afternoon and told him about her talk with Cheryl. She told him of her plan to organize the things in her bedroom like an office. He was glad she was excited, and he encouraged her to start this organization project immediately. He even offered to get her any supplies she might need for her new office. Nancy could hardly wait to get started. She knew her mother would be happy about her plan, too.

54   © Carson-Dellosa CD-2203

Name _____   Nancy's Office

Answer the questions. Circle the letter beside the correct answer.

1. Where did Nancy go after school?
   A. Cheryl's house
   B. the doctor's office
   C. her father's office
   D. a meeting

2. What did Nancy and Cheryl do while waiting for Nancy's father?
   A. They planned a surprise party for Nancy's father.
   B. They ordered office supplies for Nancy's office.
   C. They talked about Cheryl's office and how she set it up.
   D. They pretended they were movie stars.

3. Which of the following was an organization tip Cheryl gave Nancy?
   A. She told her to write neatly.
   B. She told her to throw away unnecessary things.
   C. She told her to set up a good office at her house.
   D. She told her to always be on time.

4. What did Nancy tell her father on the way home?
   A. She didn't like waiting so long.
   B. She wanted to work in an office.
   C. She wanted to organize her room like an office.
   D. She wanted Cheryl to be her new baby-sitter.

5. What did Nancy's father offer to do for her?
   A. He offered to tell Nancy's mom her plan.
   B. He offered to buy her ice cream.
   C. He offered to buy her any supplies she may need.
   D. He wanted to get her a puppy if she would care for it.

6. Who will be the next person to find out about Nancy's plan?
   A. her mother
   B. her father
   C. her teacher
   D. Cheryl

© Carson-Dellosa CD-2203 | Total Problems: | Total Correct: | Score: | 55

Name _____   The Comforts of Home

Read the passage and answer the questions on the following page.

The Comforts of Home

Robin usually rode the bus home after school. She occasionally would ride with her mom or a friend's mom in a car pool. However, this particular day was different. School had ended early due to snow. Robin was excited about the snow and wanted to go outside and play in it. But first she had to get home, and that meant riding the bus.

All of the school buses were lined up in the front driveway to wait for the children. Soon each bus would depart for a careful ride to each neighborhood on its route. Robin's house was the second stop on her bus route. After all of the buses were loaded, Robin's bus slowly rolled out onto the snowy road. The children peered anxiously out of their windows at the soft blanket of snow covering the winter countryside. After the bus pulled to a stop next to her driveway, Robin gently stepped off the bus and headed for her house.

After a sluggish walk through her snow-covered yard, Robin opened the back door of her house and entered the kitchen. The lights were on, and she smelled a pot of coffee brewing. A fire was crackling in the fireplace. Calling for her father, Robin began taking off her heavy, snow-covered coat and gloves. Soon her father came into the kitchen and greeted her with a big hug. He was very happy to see her and was relieved that she had gotten home safely. The radio and television stations had announced that the weather had caused the schools to close, and traffic delays were widespread.

Robin and her father waited for the rest of their family to arrive. Her mother's car pulled into the garage minutes later, and her older sister and mother came inside. They had been able to drive safely from the local high school where her mother is a teacher and her sister is in ninth grade. Everyone was very happy to be together. Robin suggested that they make a pot of hot cocoa and watch the snow fall outside their window. Later they could build a snowman.

56   © Carson-Dellosa CD-2203

The Comforts of Home

Name _____

Answer the questions. Circle the letter beside the correct answer.

1. Why did Robin leave school early?
   A. It was a holiday.
   (B) It was snowing.
   C. She was sick.
   D. She was going on a trip.

2. Who did Robin see when she arrived home?
   A. her mother, father, and sister
   (B) her father
   C. her mother and father
   D. her mother and sister

3. What did Robin smell in her house when she arrived home that afternoon?
   A. her mother's perfume and coffee
   B. coffee and hot chocolate
   (C) coffee
   D. pizza

4. What was the television news reporting?
   A. traffic accidents
   (B) bad weather, traffic delays, and school closings
   C. fires, bad weather, and traffic accidents
   D. school accidents and bad weather

5. Why were Robin's mother and sister at the high school?
   A. They were looking for a safe place to go in the bad weather.
   B. They decided to meet each other there.
   (C) Her mom teaches there, and her sister is a student.
   D. They both had a meeting to attend there.

6. What did Robin want to do after everyone got home?
   A. watch a movie
   (B) have hot chocolate and watch the snow fall
   C. go to bed
   D. get a puppy

Total Problems: Total Correct: Score: **57**

© Carson-Dellosa CD-2203

A New Way to Communicate

Name _____

Read the passage and answer the questions on the following page.

A New Way to Communicate

When Leslie got home from school, her father greeted her at the door. He explained that he had purchased a new computer for the family and was setting it up in the kitchen. Mr. Wilson, Leslie's father, showed her how the computer would connect to the telephone line. This would allow them to send and receive messages electronically. This is called E-mail. It is just like sending a letter, but it is much faster. Mr. Wilson explained the details of electronic mail and the Internet to his daughter. She was very interested.

Leslie asked her father several questions about the new tool, and he began to show her how it worked. He began by logging onto the Internet and then their E-mail program. They had to wait a few seconds for the connection to be made, and soon they were able to begin their transmission. Mr. Wilson explained that it is necessary to have an E-mail address in order to send or receive messages this way. Since Leslie's father has E-mail at his office, she typed a note to him and sent it with one click of the mouse!

Leslie was very excited about the E-mail possibilities at her house. She wanted to call her friend Jan to see if her family had an E-mail address and a computer. Unfortunately, Leslie remembered that Jan was out of town visiting her grandparents. She would ask her when she returned. Leslie continued to dabble at the computer using the new E-mail system. This was great fun. Leslie was amazed at how fast it could send and receive messages.

Leslie's mother and brother came home later that evening. Her brother was in high school and had a lot of experience using computers. Leslie wanted to show him how to use it, but he already knew how. Although she was a little disappointed, she was still very excited about the new communication possibilities her family now had.

58

© Carson-Dellosa CD-2203

A New Way to Communicate

Name _____

Answer the questions. Circle the letter beside the correct answer.

1. Who did Leslie send a message to?
   A. her friend Jan
   B. her mom
   (C) her dad
   D. her brother

2. Where was the family's computer set up?
   A. the den
   B. Leslie's bedroom
   (C) the kitchen
   D. her dad's office

3. Who was Mr. Wilson?
   (A) Leslie's father
   B. Leslie's teacher
   C. a neighbor
   D. Jan's father

4. What is needed to send an E-mail message?
   A. a computer, a telephone line, a mouse
   (B) an e-mail address, a telephone line, a computer
   C. the Internet, a telephone, a computer
   D. a radio, a computer, a telephone

5. Why was Leslie disappointed about her brother already knowing about E-mail?
   A. He was better at it than she was.
   (B) She was unable to show him something new.
   C. She was afraid he would use it all of the time.
   D. He had an E-mail address, and she did not.

6. With what did Leslie's brother have a lot of experience?
   (A) computers
   B. the Internet
   C. E-mail
   D. radios

Total Problems: Total Correct: Score: **59**

© Carson-Dellosa CD-2203

Dad's Surprise

Name _____

Read the passage and answer the questions. Circle the letter beside the correct answer.

Dad's Surprise

School had only been out for ten days, and John and Rebecca were already bored! They had slept late and played in the yard every day. Summer camp would not start for another week, and the weather had not been great for going to the pool. They were only allowed to watch television one hour per day. They both liked to read, but they wanted to do something really exciting.

When the children's father came home from work, he said he had a surprise for the family. He received some tickets to an amusement park from a client. The park was in a nearby city, and they could go for three days. Before he had finished telling them the news, John and Rebecca were jumping up and down with excitement.

Mr. Davis, John and Rebecca's father, said the drive to the city would take about three hours. They could stay in a hotel and go to the park each day. There were rides, shows, and places to eat there. John and Rebecca could not wait! They would be there from Thursday to Saturday.

The children got their suitcases and began to pack. John and Rebecca chatted about the trip while they gathered their clothes and shoes. This was what they had been hoping for. The summer was off to a great start!

1. What were John and Rebecca packing for?
   (A) They were going on a trip.
   B. They were going to camp.
   C. Their family was moving.
   D. They were going to their grandparents' house.

2. What had John and Rebecca been doing since school ended?
   A. playing, reading, and watching movies
   B. playing, swimming, and roller-skating
   (C) playing, sleeping late, and watching television
   D. playing, camping, and biking

3. Where did Mr. Davis get the tickets for the amusement park?
   A. He won them.
   (B) He got them from a client.
   C. He got them from a friend.
   D. He works at the park.

60   Total Problems: Total Correct: Score: © Carson-Dellosa CD-2203

© Carson-Dellosa CD-2203

Name _____   Dad's Surprise

Refer to the passage on page 60 to solve the puzzle.

Dad's Surprise Crossword Puzzle

Across

4 The family was going to this type of park
8 How many days they were going to stay
9 Where they would stay on their trip
10 The season during which this story takes place

Down

1 Where the children were going in a week
2 The children's dad had a _____ for them
3 The number between zero and two
5 Another word for fun
6 A bag for packing clothes in when you go on a trip
7 Bad _____ had prevented John and Rebecca from going to the pool

Total Problems: Total Correct: Score: **61**

© Carson-Dellosa CD-2203

Name _____   Sam and Matt

Read the passage and answer the questions on the following page.

Sam and Matt

Sam Bowers liked to climb trees, and he loved the climbing equipment at the school playground. He hoped to one day become a rock climber. He often daydreamed that he would be on the news someday because he climbed a huge mountain somewhere. But for now, Sam was in the fifth grade, and he just wanted to safely climb everything he could.

Sam was playing in his backyard one afternoon with his friend Matt. Sam decided to climb the old oak tree in the corner of his yard. Matt climbed another big tree nearby. The two boys climbed into their trees and secured themselves between two branches. They could see each other from their perches.

The boys liked being that high off the ground. Both of the boys liked their spots and decided that next time they would swap trees. Each boy took a piece of string from his pocket and tied it around a nearby branch. That way, the next time they decided to climb the trees, they would know where their spots were.

Sam's mother came to the back door and called for the boys to come inside for lunch. She was very surprised when she saw Matt and Sam climbing out of the trees. She laughed as the boys ran to the door to meet her.

62

© Carson-Dellosa CD-2203

Name _____   Sam and Matt

Answer the questions. Circle the letter beside the correct answer.

1. What did Sam like to do?
    A. play with Matt
    (B) climb things
    C. play with trees
    D. play in his backyard

2. Where did Matt go when Sam climbed a tree?
    (A) to another tree nearby
    B. to his house
    C. to Timmy's house
    D. to his soccer game

3. What did the boys plan to do differently the next time they climb the trees?
    A. wear different shoes
    B. use their two-way radios to talk
    (C) swap trees
    D. go to Matt's yard instead

4. Where did the boys go in the trees?
    A. to a secret tree house
    B. to a big limb
    (C) to a spot between two branches
    D. just to the second branch

5. What does Sam want to be when he grows up?
    A. a scientist
    (B) a rock climber
    C. a musician
    D. an astronaut

6. What reason did the boys have for getting out of the trees?
    A. It was getting dark.
    B. Mr. Bowers needed Sam's help.
    C. They were tired.
    (D) Mrs. Bowers called them for lunch.

Total Problems: Total Correct: Score: **63**

© Carson-Dellosa CD-2203

Name _____   Hockey

Read the passage and answer the questions. Circle the letter beside the correct answer.

Hockey

The national sport in Canada is ice hockey. It is a fast and exciting game played on an ice-covered rink. Each team has six players who wear ice skates and try to obtain possession of the puck. Players hold a wooden stick and try to shoot the puck past their opponents into the goal to score points. Unlike other sports, hockey allows each team to substitute players while play is in progress. This helps to maintain the game's fast pace.

A player may commit a foul with his stick or by arguing with an official. When this happens, a player may have to go to the penalty box for a set length of time or for the duration of the game. Hockey games last for sixty minutes. They are played in three segments of twenty minutes each, and the clock runs only while play is going on. Play begins with a face-off between the opposing teams. The winner is the team that scores the most points. Hockey games often end in a tie.

Hockey is fun to watch because of the speed and accuracy of the players. It is popular in the United States, Japan, and Europe, as well as in Canada.

1. Hockey is played on which type of surface?
    A. water   (B) ice
    C. clay   D. wood

2. A hockey team is made of _____ players.
    A. 5
    B. 8
    (C) 6
    D. 11

3. What rule does hockey have that other sports do not?
    A. A hockey game can end in a tie.
    B. Hockey players can argue with the officials.
    (C) Each team can substitute players while play is in progress.
    D. Hockey players usually do not wear uniforms.

4. What is the object of the game of hockey?
    A. to score a field goal   (B) to score a goal
    C. to hit the puck the fastest   D. to skate very fast

5. Which country has hockey as its national sport?
    A. United States   B. Italy
    C. Europe   (D) Canada

64   Total Problems: Total Correct: Score:

© Carson-Dellosa CD-2203

Name _____ Happiness

Read the poem and answer the questions. Circle the letter beside the correct answer.

Happiness

My dog licks my face as we roll in the grass,
I hope this playtime will slowly pass.
I slide on the floor with socks on my feet,
Mom has cleaned and it looks very neat.
On hot summer days I go to the beach,
I hope my sand castle is past the waves' reach.
My birthday begins with my breakfast of choice,
I then cheer at the ball game and lose my voice.
Bedtime is welcome to a busy kid like me,
Because I'm usually as active as one child can be.

1. What season makes the author of this poem happy?
   A. winter   (B.) summer
   C. spring   D. fall

2. Which series of words best describes the poem?
   A. birthday, homework, puppies, sunshine
   (B.) birthday, breakfast, dog, beach
   C. birthday, ball game, surfing, grades
   D. birthday, bedtime, friends, feet

3. What does the phrase "I hope my sand castle is past the waves' reach" mean?
   A. People are in the waves trying to grab the sand castle.
   B. Water will help the sand castle last a long time.
   (C.) The person does not want the water to ruin the sand castle.
   D. Ocean animals are trying to get the sand castle.

4. How does the author imply that the person in the poem is tired at the end of a day?
   A. by telling that he or she loses their voice at a ball game
   (B.) by telling that bedtime is welcome for a busy kid
   C. by telling that the person eats breakfast
   D. by telling that the person slides on the floor

5. The person described in this poem is most likely what age?
   A. 5   B. 25
   C. 2   (D.) 9

Total Problems: Total Correct: Score: **65**

© Carson-Dellosa CD-2203

Name _____ Washing Windows

Read the passage and answer the questions on the following page.

Washing Windows

Philip was looking forward to summer. He was tired of homework, book reports, and tests. He would miss seeing his friends every day at school, but that was okay. School was out, and he planned to have a lot of fun. He called his friend Tommy to plan their first outing of the summer. They decided to go bike riding and then do some batting practice at the ball field. The boys were really excited.

Just as Philip was backing his bicycle out of the garage, his mom called to him from the back door. "I need your help, Philip!" she shouted.

Philip reluctantly propped his bike by the front porch and went to see his mom. She began talking about the family's plans to do some cleaning around the house. He listened to what she was saying, and his mind was racing with thoughts of how to end his plans with Tommy. His mom had planned this "cleaning day" several weeks ago, and everyone had promised to help. Philip had forgotten about it and was very disappointed that his plans with Tommy would have to be canceled.

Philip began to mentally prepare his speech for Tommy as he went into the house. He slowly dialed Tommy's number and waited for an answer. Quickly, Philip explained that he would not be able to ride bikes and go to the ball field. Tommy was very understanding, and he asked if it would be okay if he came over to help. Philip was shocked at Tommy's request. Philip checked with his mom, and she said that would be fine. The two of them could wash the windows on the outside of the house.

When Tommy arrived, Philip was out in the front yard with a bucket of soap and water, sponges, and the hose. Tommy parked his bike and joined Philip in front of their first job, the living room window. This was the largest window in the whole house. They began working and quickly saw how their work was paying off. The windows were sparkling in the morning sun. They worked their way to the back of the house and took a break for lunch.

After the windows were cleaned, Philip's father complimented the boys on doing a great job. He offered to take the boys to the ball field for a while and then out for pizza and a movie afterward. The boys were thrilled. Perhaps washing windows wasn't so bad after all!

66

© Carson-Dellosa CD-2203

Name _____ Washing Windows

Answer the questions. Circle the letter beside the correct answer.

1. Why was Philip looking forward to summer?
   A. He wanted to get away from his friends.
   B. He was planning to get a summer job.
   (C.) He was planning to have a lot of fun.
   D. He hoped to play baseball.

2. Why did Philip have to cancel his plans with Tommy?
   A. Tommy called and said he couldn't come over.
   (B.) He had forgotten about the cleaning jobs.
   C. It was time for dinner.
   D. It was time to go inside and get ready for bed.

3. Why did Tommy go over to Philip's house?
   A. He was very good at washing windows.
   (B.) He wanted to help Philip with the cleaning.
   C. He told Philip it would be more fun to come to his house.
   D. He wanted to go to a movie.

4. What did the boys wash first?
   A. the kitchen window
   (B.) the living room window
   C. the bedroom window
   D. the hall window

5. What did Philip's father offer to the boys?
   A. an award for being the best window washers in town
   B. a trip to the movies
   C. a chance to go to a ball game
   (D.) a trip to the ball field, a movie, and a pizza

Total Problems: Total Correct: Score: **67**

© Carson-Dellosa CD-2203

Name _____ Ancient Wonders

Read the paragraph and answer the questions. Circle "True" or "False" beside each statement below.

Ancient Wonders

There are many wonderful things in our world today. Some are natural, while others are man-made. The Greeks and Romans of long ago compiled a list of things they thought were noteworthy. This list contained only man-made objects of great size or unusual quality they considered to be wonders. These objects became known as the Seven Ancient Wonders of the World. They are: the pyramids of Egypt, the Hanging Gardens of Babylon, the Temple of Artemis at Ephesus, the statue of Zeus, the Mausoleum at Halicarnassus, the Colossus of Rhodes, and the Pharos (lighthouse) of Alexandria.

1. The Seven Ancient Wonders of the World are all located in one place.   True   (False)

2. The Ancient Wonders are all man-made.   (True)   False

3. The Romans and Germans made this list of Ancient Wonders.   True   (False)

4. Only large objects or objects of unusual quality were considered wonders.   (True)   False

68   Total Problems: Total Correct: Score: © Carson-Dellosa CD-2203

Page 69

Name _____   Ancient Wonders

Refer to the passage on page 68 to solve the puzzle.

Ancient Wonders Crossword Puzzle

Crossword solution:
- 1 Down: Zeus
- 2 Across: Temple
- 3 Down: Babylon
- 4 Across: seven
- 5 Down: notsworthh (Not worth)
- 6 Down: natural
- 7 Down: wonders
- 8 Across: lighthouse
- 9 Down: Greeks
- 10 Across: Egypt

Across

2 The _____ of Artemis
4 There are _____ Ancient Wonders of the World
8 The _____ of Alexandria
10 Where the pyramids are

Down

1 One ancient wonder is a statue of this Greek god
3 The Hanging Gardens of _____
5 Another word for important or special
6 Opposite of man-made
7 Objects of great size or unusual quality were considered to be _____
9 The Romans and _____ compiled the list of wonders

© Carson-Dellosa CD-2203   Total Problems: Total Correct: Score: **69**

Page 70

Name _____   Heidi's Notebook

Read the passage and answer the questions on the following page.

Heidi's Notebook

The bell had just rung. It was eight o'clock. Kids were charging through the hall to their classes. Most of them knew running wasn't allowed, but they still ran. Heidi had put most of her things in her backpack when Neil and John ran past her. Neil's foot accidentally kicked Heidi's notebook and sent it sliding across the floor into Mr. Spencer's classroom.

Heidi stood there in amazement. Everything had happened so fast. After she gathered herself and lifted her backpack to her shoulder, she meekly walked over to Mr. Spencer's class to get her notebook. Suddenly, he closed the door to begin class. Heidi was doomed! Not only was she already late, but now she had to knock on the door to a sixth-grade teacher's class to claim her notebook.

Heidi almost got the courage to knock on the door when, to her surprise, Melinda, a sixth-grade girl she knew, opened the door. She was holding Heidi's notebook. Relieved, Heidi cheerfully greeted Melinda and thanked her for retrieving her notebook. Heidi had been rescued! She didn't have to be embarrassed in front of an entire class of sixth graders. Thank goodness for Melinda! Heidi hurried to her classroom, hoping that her teacher would understand.

70   © Carson-Dellosa CD-2203

Page 71

Name _____   Heidi's Notebook

Answer the questions. Circle the letter beside the correct answer.

1. Why did Heidi have to go to a sixth-grade classroom?
   A. She was doing a report.
   B. She had to retrieve her notebook. (circled)
   C. She was being punished.
   D. She was looking for Melinda.

2. Where was Heidi's notebook before it was kicked?
   A. in her hand
   B. on the floor (circled)
   C. in her locker
   D. in her bag

3. Who kicked Heidi's notebook?
   A. Mr. Spencer
   B. John
   C. Melinda
   D. Neil (circled)

4. Why was Heidi afraid to get her notebook?
   A. She was afraid the sixth graders would be mean or laugh.
   B. She was late to class and didn't want her teacher to know.
   C. She was hoping to get John to go get the book but was afraid to ask.
   D. She didn't want to disturb the class. (circled)

5. When did Heidi's notebook get kicked?
   A. before school started (circled)
   B. between classes
   C. after school
   D. at lunch

6. How did Melinda make Heidi feel?
   A. relieved (circled)
   B. frightened
   C. embarrassed
   D. unpopular

7. Why did the notebook get kicked?
   A. It was on the floor, and Heidi forgot about it.
   B. It was on the floor, and people were running close to it. (circled)
   C. The sixth graders were trying to play a trick on a fourth grader.
   D. There were no lockers in the school.

© Carson-Dellosa CD-2203   Total Problems: Total Correct: Score: **71**

Page 72

Name _____   Lunar Landing

Read the passage and answer the questions. Circle the letter beside the correct answer.

Lunar Landing

In 1961, the United States sent *Freedom 7* to make the first trip into space for the country. The astronaut on board was Alan Shepard, a former Navy test pilot who went on to have a long career in space travel. NASA later hired him because of his excellent pilot skills. Mr. Shepard's space flight sent him into orbit on May 5, 1961, only one month after Russia sent a man to orbit the Earth. The United States' voyage began a serious journey into the uncharted region beyond Earth.

Mr. Shepard lay on a padded fiberglass contour couch inside *Freedom 7* for his 116-mile trip beyond the Earth's surface. He returned only fifteen minutes later for a safe landing 300 miles out in the Atlantic Ocean. Ten years later, Mr. Shepard commanded the third trip to the moon for the United States on *Apollo 14*. Due to an illness, Mr. Shepard was unable to travel for the United States space program for six years. This made his return to space on *Apollo 14* that much more special and exciting. Alan Shepard was the fifth American to walk on the moon's surface.

1. Why was Alan Shepard's trip on May 5, 1961, important?
   A. It was his first trip as a pilot.
   B. It was the first space flight for the U.S. (circled)
   C. It was a very risky thing to do at that time.
   D. It became a major motion picture.

2. Where did Alan Shepard most likely get his pilot's training?
   A. Army   B. Navy (circled)
   C. Air Force   D. NASA

3. Where did Alan Shepard's trip on *Apollo 14* take him?
   A. the moon (circled)   B. Mars
   C. Pluto   D. Jupiter

4. What spacecraft did Alan Shepard command in 1971?
   A. *Apollo 14* (circled)
   B. *Apollo 13*
   C. *Freedom 7*
   D. *Freedom 8*

5. Why didn't Mr. Shepard travel into space for several years after his 1961 trip?
   A. He was scared of space travel.
   B. He was sick. (circled)
   C. He joined the Navy.
   D. He wanted to be a scientist.

72   Total Problems: Total Correct: Score: © Carson-Dellosa CD-2203

Page 73

Name _____   Lunar Landing

Refer to the passage on page 72 to solve the puzzle.

Lunar Landing Crossword Puzzle

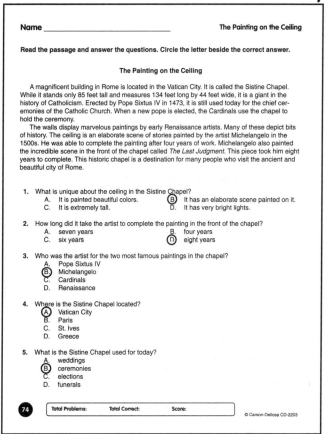

Across

3 Alan Shepard commanded this trip to the moon on *Apollo 14*
5 A person who travels into space
9 This country sent a man into space one month before the U.S.
10 Shepard landed in this ocean after his mission in *Freedom 7*

Down

1 Shepard was the _____ American to walk on the moon
2 To travel around
4 The planet on which we live
6 The region beyond the Earth
7 To come back again
8 Shepard was a former Navy _____

Total Problems: _____ Total Correct: _____ Score: _____   **73**

Page 74

Name _____   The Painting on the Ceiling

Read the passage and answer the questions. Circle the letter beside the correct answer.

The Painting on the Ceiling

A magnificent building in Rome is located in the Vatican City. It is called the Sistine Chapel. While it stands only 85 feet tall and measures 134 feet long by 44 feet wide, it is a giant in the history of Catholicism. Erected by Pope Sixtus IV in 1473, it is still used today for the chief ceremonies of the Catholic Church. When a new pope is elected, the Cardinals use the chapel to hold the ceremony.

The walls display marvelous paintings by early Renaissance artists. Many of these depict bits of history. The ceiling is an elaborate scene of stories painted by the artist Michelangelo in the 1500s. He was able to complete the painting after four years of work. Michelangelo also painted the incredible scene in the front of the chapel called *The Last Judgment*. This piece took him eight years to complete. This historic chapel is a destination for many people who visit the ancient and beautiful city of Rome.

1. What is unique about the ceiling in the Sistine Chapel?
    A. It is painted beautiful colors.   (B) It has an elaborate scene painted on it.
    C. It is extremely tall.   D. It has very bright lights.

2. How long did it take the artist to complete the painting in the front of the chapel?
    A. seven years   B. four years
    C. six years   (D) eight years

3. Who was the artist for the two most famous paintings in the chapel?
    A. Pope Sixtus IV
    (B) Michelangelo
    C. Cardinals
    D. Renaissance

4. Where is the Sistine Chapel located?
    (A) Vatican City
    B. Paris
    C. St. Ives
    D. Greece

5. What is the Sistine Chapel used for today?
    A. weddings
    (B) ceremonies
    C. elections
    D. funerals

74 Total Problems: _____ Total Correct: _____ Score: _____

Page 75

Name _____   The Painting on the Ceiling

Refer to the passage on page 74 to solve the puzzle.

The Painting on the Ceiling Crossword Puzzle

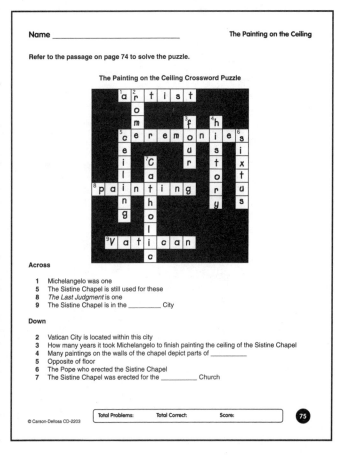

Across

1 Michelangelo was one
5 The Sistine Chapel is still used for these
8 *The Last Judgment* is one
9 The Sistine Chapel is in the _____ City

Down

2 Vatican City is located within this city
3 How many years it took Michelangelo to finish painting the ceiling of the Sistine Chapel
4 Many paintings on the walls of the chapel depict parts of _____
5 Opposite of floor
6 The Pope who erected the Sistine Chapel
7 The Sistine Chapel was erected for the _____ Church

Total Problems: _____ Total Correct: _____ Score: _____   **75**

Page 76

Name _____   Honeybees

Read the passage and answer the questions on the following page.

Honeybees

Honeybees are interesting creatures. They are capable of giving painful stings to humans, but they also provide honey. In fact, they are the only insect that makes a product humans can consume. The organization of the bee community is highly sophisticated. All of the tasks are distributed among the members of the colony, or group, in order to efficiently carry out the work.

Within a colony, scientists have discovered one queen, several drones, and a lot of worker bees. The queen is not responsible for any of the work. The queen is always a very large female and does not even get her own food. That is done for her. She is responsible for the reproduction of the colony. She mates several times a year and produces many offspring. If the queen is not in the hive, the other bees become disorganized and anxious. The queen's fertilized eggs become worker bees, while the unfertilized eggs become drones.

Worker bees are female, and they are always busy gathering food and caring for the young. At a very early age they begin to go out and gather nectar for the hive. No matter how long the trip takes to find food or how far away from the hive the bee is, the route the worker takes back to the hive is the shortest. That is how the term "beeline" came about.

The males are called drones, and they do not work. They are responsible for mating and protecting the queen while the workers gather food. They live only a short time. In autumn, the workers let the drones starve to death because they are no longer useful, and they would eat too much honey during the winter.

76

Name _____   Honeybees

Answer the questions. Write a "T" next to each statement that is true. Write an "F" if the statement is false.

1. _F_ Worker bees are males and females.

2. _T_ The queen keeps the colony organized.

3. _F_ Most of the worker bees die in autumn.

4. _T_ Drones are male honeybees.

5. _T_ Honey made by honeybees is suitable for humans to eat.

Answer the questions below. Circle the letter beside the correct answer.

6. What are the duties of the queen honeybee?
   A. mating, building the hive, protecting the young
   B. mating and keeping the hive organized and busy
   C. gathering food, making honey, and mating
   D. mating and protecting the hive

7. Why do the worker bees travel in a beeline?
   A. The queen expects them to.
   B. It is the shortest distance back to the hive.
   C. They line up behind one another.
   D. They cannot all go into the hive at one time.

8. Which words best describe worker bees?
   A. large, weak, hungry
   B. large, lazy, clumsy
   C. fast, mean, tired
   D. hardworking, busy, caring

9. The queen's eggs become worker bees when:
   A. the eggs are not fertilized
   B. the honey flow is over
   C. the eggs have been fertilized
   D. the weather is cooler

© Carson-Dellosa CD-2203

| Total Problems: | Total Correct: | Score: |

77

Name _____   Honeybees

Refer to the passage on page 76 to solve the puzzle.

Honeybees Crossword Puzzle

Across

3 A bee community is called this
6 A type of bee that makes honey
8 A male who protects the queen
9 Drones starve during this season
10 A bug or bee is this type of animal

Down

1 Honeybees make this
2 A bee who reproduces young for the colony
4 Bees gather this to make honey
5 A female who gathers food
7 The gender of all worker bees

78

| Total Problems: | Total Correct: | Score: |

© Carson-Dellosa CD-2203

© Carson-Dellosa CD-2203